PsychoSophical

Embracing the Paradox of Inner Reality

Ayesha Singh

BookLeaf Publishing
India | USA | UK

Made with ❤ on the BookLeaf Publishing Platform
www.bookleafpub.in
www.bookleafpub.com

Dedication

To my beloved husband, whose gentle light ignited the spark of my muse and transformed silent whispers into verses;
To my dearest brother—Mom and Dad—whose unwavering spirit shines like a guiding light through every storm;
To my cherished family, whose boundless love guides me like a steadfast star;
And to the silent souls whose hope lit my darkest nights, to every wandering heart that finds solace in these lines.
This collection is a tribute to those who dare to listen to their inner voice, embracing every scar and celebrating the splendour of life.
May each ending cradle the promise of a new dawn, and every shadow gently yield to the light of endless possibility.

Preface

In the silent spaces between waking and dreaming, where the mundane dissolves into mystery, there lies a vast inner universe waiting to be discovered. *PsychoSophical* is a journey into that hidden realm—a collection of 51 poems that traverse the shifting landscapes of the mind and heart. Here, personal myth meets philosophy; every shadow conceals a spark of light, and every fragment of memory whispers a timeless truth.

These verses emerged from moments of deep introspection, when the quiet voices of the past collided with the promise of a new dawn. They are born of vulnerability—of embracing both our scars and our splendour—and they transform the weight of memory into a beacon of hope. From the reflective murmurings of a silent mirror to the steady pulse of a guiding compass, each poem maps the contours of a soul in constant evolution, a soul that seeks to reconcile the myriad fragments of its being.

Drawing inspiration from my own journey through loss, joy, and transformation, I have sought to capture the beauty inherent in our imperfect, transient existence.

The imagery—an unfaltering clock in a still room, a delicate feather kindling new beginnings, a labyrinth of memories that both haunt and heal—serves as a metaphor for our endless quest for meaning and self-acceptance.

Interwoven with expressions in both English and Hindi, these poems speak a universal language that bridges cultures and generations. They remind us that while our paths may diverge, the yearning for inner truth, the embrace of our vulnerabilities, and the desire to rise from our deepest trials are experiences we all share.

PsychoSophical is not a manual offering tidy answers; it is a tapestry of soulful reflections—a gentle invitation to pause, listen, and rediscover the resilient light that dwells within. May these pages guide you to unearth your hidden truths, mend your fractured dreams, and inspire you to live with an open heart, knowing that every moment of stillness carries the seed of transformation.

Welcome to this introspective odyssey. May you find courage in your reflections, wisdom in your scars, and the unwavering hope to rise with every new dawn.

Acknowledgements

This book is a tapestry of my inner journey—a mosaic of moments, both luminous and shadowed, woven with threads of hope, despair, and transformation. Every verse is a step along an uncharted path, a quiet celebration of the courage to face oneself in the rawest form. I extend my deepest gratitude to all who have illuminated my path and helped shape these pages into a true reflection of the soul.

To my dearest husband, Sankalp, and my beloved brother, Shubham—your unwavering faith, brilliance, and quiet encouragement have breathed life into my words. Sankalp, you have been my steady light, guiding me through the labyrinth of self-doubt with tenderness and strength. Shubham, your steadfast belief in my journey has been the foundation upon which every word stands, inspiring me to rise even in the darkest hours.

To my loving parents and cherished family, your boundless love has nurtured every spark of creativity. Your constant support has lifted me in moments of vulnerability, celebrated every small victory, and reminded me that even in darkness there is always a glimmer of light to guide us home.

To my dear friends—whose honest reflections, late-night musings, and unwavering kindness have enriched this journey—you have been the gentle chorus that transformed pain into art. Your presence has been a soothing balm in my solitude, teaching me to see beauty in imperfection and to cherish the raw, unfiltered moments of life.

To my mentors and teachers, who unveiled the worlds of literature, philosophy, and art before me—you have shown me that vulnerability is not a weakness, but a profound strength. Your wisdom has ignited a passionate fire within, proving that the courage to voice one's truth is the ultimate act of defiance in a world often cloaked in pretense.

I also extend my heartfelt gratitude to the quiet souls who have left their mark on my life—each a silent beacon of resilience and grace. Your untold stories, your simple acts of kindness, and your quiet perseverance resonate deeply within these pages.

And finally, to every reader who journeys through these verses—thank you for finding echoes of your own heart within these lines. May this collection invite you to explore your inner landscapes, honour your imperfections, and find solace in the shared dance of existence. I am forever grateful to the universe for gifting me the capacity for introspection and the courage to confront my own shadows, for it is in that delicate space between darkness and light that our truest selves are revealed.

Together, may we continue to embrace the beauty of transformation and find strength in every chapter of our unfolding stories.

1. The Mirror's Whisper

It began at the stroke of midnight,
A hush in the corridor of my own making.
A single candle stood guard, quivering in the dark,
Casting unsettled shapes upon the walls.
I faced the silent mirror, already feeling its pull.

In that silvered surface, I saw not just my face
But the ghosts of every choice I tried to outrun.
Each movement, each breath, became a question mark:
Who am I behind these practiced expressions?
Why do I fear the truth I sense forming on my lips?
What secrets lie hidden in the depths of this reflection?

The mirror whispered softly at first—
A chime of distant bells echoing inside my chest.
It spoke of lost hopes, broken promises,
Dreams deferred and illusions worn like armour.
With each word, the reflection gained depth and life.

I flinched as hidden memories flooded in—
The way I lied to my younger self,
The way I drowned regret in hollow laughter,
The way I let the world's noise become my lullaby.
Yet the whisper persisted, peeling away my masks.

I reached out, desperate to hush this unyielding voice.
But the glass was cool, unwavering, unstoppable.
In its unwavering gaze, I recognized my own exhaustion:
Yearning for an embrace that needs no pretenses,
Longing for a moment where all shadows turn to light.

In that final hour before dawn broke, I surrendered.
The mirror held my story, blemishes and all—
No more turning away, no more shallow illusions.
Its whisper became my own voice, woven with honesty,
And in that unison, I found the seed of acceptance.

"आईने की गिरह में छुपी थी मेरी सच्चाई,
एक-एक परत खुलती गई, जैसे सुबह की उजास।
खुद से नज़रें चुराने का सिलसिला हुआ ख़त्म,
आज मैं अपने होने को पूरी तरह गले लगाती हूँ—
रहस्य नहीं, मैं ही हूँ अपना प्रकाश।"

2. The Digital Beacon

In the hum of the neon city,
Amid the buzz of screens and restless networks,
A soft glow emerges—a digital beacon,
A subtle pulse beneath the urban din,
Whispering of hidden truths waiting to be found.

Amid concrete jungles and pixelated skies,
The beacon calls like a gentle algorithm,
Guiding a modern wanderer through data streams,
Past the static of everyday noise,
Into a realm where inner light meets virtual wonder.

Navigating back alleys of coded memories,
They uncover forgotten files and archived dreams,
Each click and scroll a step deeper into self,
Unraveling layers of digital echoes,
Transforming bits of the past into sparks of insight.

Under the soft glow of glowing billboards,
The seeker discovers a hidden app of reflection,
Where words once typed on tired keys transform
Into a mosaic of personal revelations,
Illuminating the dark corners of their modern soul.

Through virtual corridors and encrypted thoughts,
The beacon unlocks portals to inner sanctuaries,
Where every challenge in the digital maze
Becomes a lesson in resilience and hope,
And every error message reveals a chance to evolve.

Amid constant connection and fleeting distraction,
The digital beacon offers a pause—a moment of calm,
Inviting the seeker to step away from the noise,
To breathe and decode the silent language within,
Where the data of the heart reveals its timeless code.

As dawn creeps over the city's horizon,
The beacon's light softens, yet remains unwavering,
A reminder that even amidst the digital whirlwind,
True illumination lies in embracing one's own story,
A quiet resolve shining through the modern maze.

"अब इस डिजिटल दुनिया में,
जहाँ हर सूचना में बसी है एक नई दास्ताँ,
वहाँ एक ज्वलंत चिराग जलता है,
जो आत्मा की गहराई से अपनी कहानी सुनाता है,
सच्ची रोशनी वही है,
जो दिल के डेटा में असीम ऊर्जा जगाती है।"

3. The Labyrinth of Memory

I stumbled upon a corridor of echoes,
A doorway hidden behind the folds of night.
My heart pounded like a distant drum,
A silent whisper urged me onward,
Guiding me into a maze woven from obscured dreams.
I called it curiosity; the walls whispered otherwise—
It was longing, regret, a need for answers.

Each turn led me deeper into the labyrinth,
Where memories surfaced like lost ships at sea.
In one corner, I saw a child crying for comfort
While I stood frozen in self-doubt.
In another, a friend's outstretched hand
I was too proud to grasp.
I felt the air grow thick with unspoken apologies.

Torches flickered along the winding path,
Casting shadows of the person I used to be.
I chased the silhouettes, along the endless path,
Hoping to catch them,
To say the words I never found before.
Yet each time I grew closer, they dissolved
Back into the labyrinth's secret corners.

A distant bell chimed—once, twice, a thousand times—
Time was fluid, bending around my unresolved past.
I heard the faint sob of a heart once broken,
The echo of laughter that refused to fade.
Each fragment tugged at my sleeves like a plea,
Asking to be seen, to be felt, to be freed,
A hidden rhythm pulsed through the silence.

At last, I reached a small clearing at the centre,
An open space where silence greeted me.
No mirrors, no illusions, just stillness
That brought a wave of understanding.
I knelt on the cold stone floor,
Releasing every guilt, every "If Only,"
And offered them to the hush of the labyrinth.

"नीरवता के उस मध्य में, मैंने ख़ुद को पाया,
अतीत के हर आँसू और अधूरी पुकार ने दी आवाज़।
गिरहें खुलीं, मन हल्का हुआ—एक नए सूरज का वादा,
क्षमा का दीप जल उठा, और राहों ने अपना बोझ उतार दिया।
अब हर मोड़ पर स्मृतियाँ हैं, पर बोझ नहीं—मैं आज़ाद हूँ।"

4. The Tempest Within

In the quiet of a bright, clear night,
A gentle storm began to stir—
Not of despair, but of vibrant energy
And creative spark.
Thunder became a rhythmic beat,
Echoing like a joyful drum,
Lightning revealed dazzling patterns
Of inner brilliance,
And a refreshing tempest danced within,
Awakening new light.
The breeze whispered secrets of untold dreams,
While the sky shimmered with promise of fresh
beginnings.

Waves of passionate energy surged
Across my inner horizon,
Each thought blossomed with the promise
Of untamed possibility.
My mind transformed into a vibrant stage
Of harmonious forces,
Where hope and determination twirled together
In brilliant display,
And every heartbeat pulsed with the thrill
Of renewed spirit.

Stars blinked softly as silent witnesses
To my rebirth,
As the cosmos cheered the rise of dreams
In their purest form.

Amid the lively swirl, treasured memories
Sparkled like fireflies,
Old joys and warm laughter lit up
The corridors of my soul.
Every recollection shone with the colours
Of love and inspiration,
Soft echoes of delightful moments
Painted a mural of inner bliss,
And each memory became a stepping stone
To newfound happiness.

The storm's powerful roar gave way
To a playful, uplifting energy,
Transforming chaos into a symphony
Of radiant emotions.
Each surge of passion filled me
With the courage to celebrate life,
Channeling every burst of energy
Into a beacon of creative hope,
Illuminating the path ahead
With joy and unwavering optimism.

In the calm that followed, a gentle stillness
Embraced my soul,
Offering a sanctuary where dreams
And laughter intertwined.
I paused to feel the warm glow
Of inner peace and contentment,
Realizing that every challenge
Had led to this bright, renewed state,
A joyful reminder that even storms
Can spark a happy transformation.

"अब इस तूफ़ान में भी,
जहाँ हर बिजली उम्मीद की किरणें बिखेरती है,
मेरी आत्मा ने हँसना और खिलना सीखा है,
हर लहर में नई खुशियों की धुन गूँजती है,
और हर अँधेरे में अटल साहस की चमक झलकती है।
यह मेरे जीवन का उजाला है—
एक अटूट मुस्कान,
जो हर तूफ़ान के बाद,
और भी तेज़, प्रखर बन उठती है।"

5. The Painted Mask

A silent tension coils beneath chandelier light,
Where guests glide like phantoms in satin and silk.
The orchestra's waltz pulses through marble floors,
Yet I sense another rhythm—a tide of watchful eyes.

My mask gleams with painted gold and crimson,
Hiding every waver of doubt etched in my brow.
The crowd's glances flicker, part curiosity, part suspicion,
I wonder who truly sees my fear's shape.

I weave between swirling gowns and velvet coats,
Shadows dancing at the periphery of my vision.
A hush of whispers snakes along the walls,
Each rumour more chilling than the last:
"Who is she, really?"
"What secrets lie beneath that painted facade?"
"And what truth lies hidden behind that elusive smile?"

Thunder rumbles in the distance—
The storm outside mirrors the one in my chest.
Lightning flashes through stained-glass windows,
Momentarily illuminating every crack on my mask.
In that brief shock of light, a figure steps forward,
Eyes fixated, daring me to uncloak my truth.

The music falters, replaced by an electric hush,
A hush thick enough to taste.
I feel the weight of unspoken questions swirling,
Answers clawing at my throat, desperate to be free.
A single violin note hangs in the air like a final plea,
Urging me to unmask or vanish forever.

With trembling fingers, I trace the gilded edges—
Paint peeling, illusions crumbling, heart pounding.
Dread tangles with a strange, fierce hope:
To reveal myself might be ruinous,
But continuing this masquerade feels far worse.
My breath catches—and I cast the mask aside.

"बिजलियों के गर्जन में, झूठी सजावटें झरने लगीं,
सियाह रात की ख़ामोशी में, सबकी नज़रें एकटक टिक गईं।
धड़कते दिलों के बीच, हक़ीक़त ने दी एक दस्तक,
चेहरा बेपर्दा हुआ, और हर भ्रम टूटकर बिखर गया—
आज से मेरा सच ही मेरा अभिमान है।"

6. The Tattered Journal

Tucked away in a dust-laden attic,
I unearth the journal's frayed binding.
Threads dangle from the spine like forgotten tales,
Waiting for light after years lost in shadows.
Its cover bears faint scribbles of a name,
Barely recognizable—yet undeniably mine.

The first pages quiver with childish scrawls,
A forest of misspelled dreams and fantasies.
I see myself, wide-eyed and fearless,
Writing down hopes as though the world were infinite.
Crayon sunbursts bleed into shimmering lakes,
Where monsters and angels coexist in pastel harmony.

Between these pages, a faded photograph appears,
Its edges softened by time's gentle hand.
A captured smile, a whisper of past delight,
Holding memories of sunlit, forgotten days.
In that silent image, echoes of youth reside,
A secret kept safe in ink and paper.

Midway through, penmanship transforms—
Adolescent anguish sears the paper's edges.
There are tear-blotted lines of heartbreak,

Angry confessions scrawled at midnight,
A longing to be seen, understood, forgiven.
In each trembling sentence, a raw, electric truth.

Flicking forward, I find pages where reality blurs,
Where the ink blossoms into surreal tangents:
My future self meeting old regrets in a dreamscape,
Stars rearranging themselves to form a secret message,
Moments in which time loops back on itself,
As if memory and imagination were twin mirrors.

The book crackles with an uneasy magic,
A testament to the fragility of honesty.
Each word, a window to who I once was—
Each margin, a portal to who I might become.
I feel the weight of confessions laid bare,
Tempted to tear them yet compelled to keep them close.

In the hush of this attic twilight,
I sense the journal's silent plea:
To accept every version of me across its tattered pages,
Neither condemning the naive nor erasing the broken.
For in these intimate scribbles lies a quiet courage,
A willingness to face the unvarnished self.

Closing the cover, I inhale dust and resolution.
Maybe the words were never perfect—

But perfection isn't the point;
It's the telling, the grappling with raw truths,
That breathes life into fading ink and brittle pages.
And perhaps, in sharing my stories,
I find the power to rewrite what comes next.

"इन मुड़े-तुड़े पन्नों में, मेरी साँसों का अक्स बसता है,
बचपन के सपनों से लेकर आज की उलझनों तक—सब यहाँ दर्ज हैं।
शब्दों के ये धागे ही तो हैं, जो भूत और भविष्य को बाँधते हैं,
और इसी कच्चे इक़रार में छिपी है मेरी सबसे गहरी आज़ादी—
क्योंकि असल ख़ूबसूरती इसी बेचैन सच्चाई में बसी है।"

7. The Dancer at Dusk

There she stands at the water's edge,
A solitary figure against a violet sky.
The sun bleeds into the horizon,
Waves hush their roar to witness her grace.
She moves, and the sand beneath her feet
Seems to glow with the final embers of day.

Her arms arch like questions to the heavens,
Fingers trailing unseen paths in the air.
Every pivot, every gentle leap,
Tells a tale of moments slipping by.
A fragile hush lies between her heartbeats,
A fleeting pause where time itself exhales.

I watch from a distance, transfixed—
Wondering if she embodies the sunset's farewell.
For each swirl of her skirt conjures illusions:
Sunbeams echo in the dusk,
Shadows stretch out like longing memories,
And a reflection of who she once was blooms and fades.

Philosophers speak of impermanence—
That all beauty crumbles into dust or foam.
Yet in her dancing, I see a quiet defiance:

A testament that within the moment's brevity,
There lies an entire universe of feeling
Poised to vanish as swiftly as it arrives.

Her footprints vanish under the tide's gentle push,
As though time itself cannot abide permanence.
There is a hush in her expression,
A tear that sparkles in the twilight glow.
We sense her joy, her mourning for each second passing,
Her acceptance that every breath must be let go.

Waves roll on, persistent and ancient,
Carrying the echoes of vanished civilizations.
She dances on, unbroken by the knowledge
That her stage will soon be swallowed by night.
A silent vow in every step: to embrace the ephemeral,
To live in the hush before the darkness claims the day.

In this fragile interplay of light and shadow,
I glimpse the heartbeat of existence itself—
Transient, unstoppable, achingly real.
Her dance is a language beyond words,
A tapestry woven from twilight's fleeting colours,
Surrendered to the relentless pull of time.

When the final sliver of sun sinks below the horizon,
She ends with a spin, hair brushing salt-kissed breeze.

In that hush, I sense she holds a truth:
We are all dancers under fading skies,
Carving our stories in sand that the next tide will erase--
Yet the beauty lives in the dance, not its permanence.

"शाम की आख़िरी रोशनी में,
उसके कदम उभारते अनकहे अफसाने।
हर पल चुपचाप निशान बिखेर जाता है,
जैसे वक्त की रेत में मिलते अधूरे ख्वाब।
लहरों ने तो पगचिन्ह मिटा दिए,
पर हर लहर में गूंजता है दर्द और उम्मीद का स्वर।
क्षणभंगुरता में छुपा है अनंत अनुभव,
जहाँ हर सांस में ज़िंदगी का नया सवेरा चमकता है।"

8. The Pilgrim's Odyssey

In a vast, barren land, a solitary pilgrim
Embarks on a quiet odyssey.
The wind murmurs ancient secrets,
Carrying whispers of forgotten lore.
Each step becomes a silent prayer,
A call for meaning in an endless expanse.
Guided by nature's unspoken wisdom,
The pilgrim moves with humble resolve,
Venturing into solitude
Where the sky stretches beyond measure.

The earth unfolds like a rugged canvas—
Hills and dusty plains in stark contrast.
In the stillness, the pilgrim listens
To the murmur of ancient stones.
Each footfall is a sacred offering
To the silent power of the land.
Amid desolation, a fragile light glows—
A beacon of quiet endurance,
Illuminating the journey
With the promise of hidden strength.

Beneath a sky brushed with fading twilight,
The pilgrim finds a gentle respite.

Shadows and soft streams echo
With nature's tender lullaby,
Revealing a language of inner calm
That soothes the wandering soul.
In that moment, the earth speaks
Through rustling leaves and whispered water,
And the pilgrim's heart awakens
To the hymn of renewal and hope.

As the path winds onward,
Mirages of doubt shimmer in the distance,
Yet every challenge carves a deeper resolve
In the pilgrim's spirit.
Step by step, uncertainty transforms
Into a radiant beacon of light,
Illuminating the rugged path
Toward self-realization
And igniting a quiet fire
That propels the wanderer ever forward.

In each pause, the pilgrim reflects
On echoes of past trials—
Scars of old struggles mingling
With the courage of newfound dreams.
The barren land mirrors a soul in transition,
Revealing hidden reservoirs of strength.
Every stride becomes a chapter

In a story of transformation
And quiet triumph,
Etching a legacy of resilience
Into the timeless landscape.

At the horizon's edge,
A gentle glow emerges like a promise reborn—
A soft radiance signaling both inner light
And tender renewal.
The pilgrim pauses, heart awash in serene wonder,
Realizing that every step was a sacred lesson
In the art of becoming,
And that the journey itself
Is the key to uncovering the true self.

"अब इस सुनसान धरती के हर कोने में,
जहाँ हर कदम खुदा की दुआ की तरह गूंजता है,
और हवाओं में रूह की सदा गूंजती है।
मौन की गहराई में छिपे अनदेखे रहस्य,
धीरे-धीरे अपनी परछाइयों में प्रकट होते हैं,
जैसे अंधेरों में चाँद की किरणें उजाला बिखेरती हैं।
इस एकांत यात्रा में हर पल नयी पहचान को जन्म देता है,
हर धड़कन में प्रतिबिंबित होती है
सच्ची पहचान की अमर दास्ताँ,
जो टूटे सपनों को फिर से सजग करती है
और वीरानी में आशा की लौ जगाती है।"

9. The Lighthouse Keeper

Beyond the jagged rocks and unrelenting tide,
I stand in a lonely tower, night after night.
My lantern's beam rips through the howling dark,
Protecting distant vessels from unseen peril.
Yet in my own reflection, I find little solace.

They call me a saviour, a silent hero of the coast,
But heroism can mask a hidden longing.
Each ship that passes by finds refuge in my light,
Unaware that my own spirit drifts aimless,
Haunted by shadows I cannot repel.

I question the purpose of a beacon that never rests,
Its brilliance unwavering, a vigil for others.
Am I the flame, destined only to illuminate,
Or the moth, circling in search of a glow I cannot feel?
I wrestle with these thoughts like an eternal tide.

Memories line the walls of this tower—
Missed chances, letters, the weight of unspoken truths.
Sometimes I hear them echo in the silence,
In each muted whisper, I face the cost of solitude,
Like waves crashing endlessly against my mind:
They remind me that saving others has not saved me.

The sea, vast and indifferent, mirrors my internal void:
Restless, boundless, cloaked in deep uncertainty.
At times I dream of plunging into its cold embrace,
Hoping to find clarity in the underwater hush,
Yet I remain anchored by the flicker of duty.

Philosophers speak of guiding lights, of noble callings,
But do they speak of loneliness that gnaws at the soul?
In these windswept hours before dawn,
I wonder if every guiding hand needs a guide,
If every torch thirsts for its own spark of hope.

Then daybreak creeps upon the horizon,
Pastel colours melting through the foggy gloom.
I shield tired eyes from rays of warmth,
Realizing that maybe—just maybe—this quiet sacrifice
Is a language of empathy, too profound for simple words.

"बंद दरवाज़ों में छिपी अनकही कहानियों की तरह,
मैं भी अपने उजाले और अँधेरे के बीच भटकता हूँ।
और फिर भी, दूर समंदर में भटकती हर नाव के लिए,
ये रौशनी बन जाती है उनका आख़िरी किनारा—
शायद इसी विरक्ति में ही, मुझे अपना अर्थ मिलना था।"

10. The Unbound Soul

A spirit once confined by silent chains,
Bound by society's rigid expectations,
Lived in the shadow of a prescribed role,
Its light dimmed by constant judgment,
Yearning for the freedom of its true self.

One day, a spark of defiance ignited within,
Whispers of hope stirred deep in its core,
The invisible bonds began to shatter,
Each broken link a step toward liberation,
As the spirit realized its inner strength.

With trembling resolve, it broke free,
Soaring upward into an open, endless sky,
Where possibilities stretched beyond the horizon,
The chains of conformity left far behind,
And freedom sang in every breath of wind.

In that vast expanse, self-discovery unfolded,
Every flutter of its wings revealed hidden truths,
Embracing every scar and shadow of the past,
The soul learned that vulnerability breeds power,
And that every facet of its being was worthy.

As it journeyed through radiant skies,
The unbound soul met both light and storm,
Each trial a lesson in self-acceptance,
Transforming pain into a quiet triumph,
And doubt into the courage to shine.

The world below faded into distant memory,
Replaced by a mosaic of newfound colours and dreams,
The spirit danced with the winds of possibility,
Finding solace in the embrace of its own truth,
A celebration of all that it was meant to be.

In every soaring moment, the soul felt alive,
Freed from the weight of external expectations,
It revealed in the beauty of its imperfection,
Every heartbeat echoed its radiant autonomy,
A reminder that freedom comes from within.

The journey transformed into a luminous odyssey,
Where each step deepened self-love and understanding,
The unbound soul learned to honour every flaw,
Finding in its liberated flight a profound peace,
A testament to the power of embracing one's entirety.

In the vast openness, the soul basks in freedom,
Every breath a renewal of its limitless spirit,
It glides on winds of possibility and dreams,

Leaving behind echoes of a confining past,
Embracing a future filled with radiant potential.

"अब ये अनंत आकाश में उड़ता है,
जहाँ हर पल में बसता है सच्चा आत्मविश्वास,
हर टूटे हुए बंधन से मिलती है नई राह,
और हर धड़कन गुनगुनाती है, खुद को अपनाने का संदेश।
यह स्वतंत्र आत्मा हमें सिखाती है, कि असली आज़ादी
अपने आप को पूरी तरह से स्वीकार करने में है।"

11. The Sacred Accord

Deep within ancient caves,
Vibrant murals and carved stone murmur unity
In hushed tones of timeless mystery.
Worn walls echo voices
That once celebrated eternal bonds,
Now bathed in steadfast, quiet light.
A modern wanderer steps into this living archive,
Immersed in secrets etched in stone.

Driven by restless curiosity and the pulse of digital age,
He enters cool, shadowed corridors
Where the past meets the present.
Fingertips trace inscriptions spanning eras,
Each groove a testament to shared human dreams
Bridging what was with what may be.
Reflections flicker like brief lightning
On ancient walls merging with modern glow.
Under shifting light and soft neon hues,
Frescoes burst into a vibrant symphony of colour.
The carvings whisper tales of joy and sorrow,
Of hearts that beat as one
Even as time and technology reshape our world.
The stone awakens as a canvas for visionary souls,
Each shadow and glimmer pulsing with resilience.

In this sacred accord, insight surges like a tidal wave,
As ancient wisdom converges with contemporary hope.
The cave transforms into a sanctuary
Where digital dreams and age-old truths meet,
Offering renewal and creative transformation.
Every step becomes a revelation,
Each moment a spark illuminating the path ahead.

"अब इन प्राचीन गुफाओं की गहराइयों में,
जहाँ हर नक़्क़ाशी एक अविस्मरणीय कहानी कहती है,
हर छाप में उजागर होती है आशा की अनंत लौ,
जो पुराने रागों से लेकर नए स्वप्नों का संगम है।
यहाँ पत्थरों की कठोरता में भी प्रेम का ज्वाला जलता है,
और हर रेखा हमें याद दिलाती है कि हम सब एक हैं।
इस एकता में छुपा है अपार साहस और अटूट विश्वास,
जो अंधेरों को चीरते हुए नयी सुबह की ओर ले जाता है।
यह परम संदेश है हमारे अस्तित्व का,
जो हमें अनंत शांति और उजाले की ओर अग्रसर करता है।"

12. The Perpetual Hourglass

In a dim-lit study, tucked behind dusty tomes,
I find an hourglass gleaming with an otherworldly glow.
Its glass walls seem too perfect, its sand ever shifting.
A hush surrounds it, as though holding its breath,
Waiting for a curious hand to tilt it once again.
Its silent allure beckons me into mystery.
I turn it over—sand cascades with rhythmic grace,
Yet it never seems to deplete.
With every gentle flip, a new era awakens:
Pharaohs rise and crumble into legends,
Forgotten empires resurrect in swirling grains,
And the present dissolves into a tapestry of lost hours.
Each grain a silent witness to ages untold,
Whispering secrets of futures yet to unfold.

Each epoch etched in shifting sand stirs questions:
Is time a straight line that we traverse only once,
Or a circle retraced by our echoes?
I watch centuries drift in the hush between heartbeats,
As if the glass walls hold a cosmic secret,
A story of beginnings that never truly end.
I feel the weight of civilizations pressing against my soul,
The silent plea of ghosts who marched across seasons.
Within this dance of sand, I sense my smallness—

A single note in an endless composition,
Where every measure is essential yet fleeting.
Yet in each fleeting moment, my spirit finds its echo.
In the echo of time, I find both sorrow and wonder,
A reminder that life's rhythm is both fleeting and eternal.

Curiosity spurs me to flip the glass faster,
Hoping to outrun destiny, to rewrite outcomes.
But time remains indifferent, swirling steadily on,
Reshaping illusions, forging new silhouettes.
The final grain never falls; the cycle never breaks.
In its endless spiral, fate whispers an eternal refrain.
Is it mercy or torment that this clock never empties?
To watch epochs reborn could inspire awe—
Or erode hope, as each story mirrors the last.
I trace a finger along the cool glass,
Seeking an answer in its unblinking stillness,
Yet the only response is the endless, silent cascade.
And in that cascade, destiny reveals its hidden cadence,
A quiet promise that each moment births a new horizon.

My reflection in that glass reveals a shifting face,
Youth to age, clarity to doubt, and back again.
I realize we all exist in these eternal flips,
Bound by invisible threads of memory and prophecy.
The hourglass is but a symbol of our restless longing,
To claim mastery over time, even as it slips away.

Yet in that silence, where time and memory converge,
I glimpse a future whispered in each lingering grain.
A cosmic dance of possibility and fate unfolds,
Merging all that was, is, and might yet be.
In this eternal cycle, my heart finds solace and query—
For within the shifting sands, we are forever reborn.
In that mirror, I see the fusion of past and promise,
A reminder that renewal lies in every shifting grain.

"जब रेत का हर कण नई कहानी कहता है,
तब समझ आता है—समय कभी रुकता नहीं, बस रूप बदलता है।
हर बूंद में छुपी होती है अनकही दास्ताँ,
जो याद दिलाती है, जीवन का चक्र चलता रहता है।
वक़्त के इस नर्तन में, हम सब मौन दर्शक हैं,
हर पल जीते हैं, हर पल मिट जाते हैं।
इस निरंतर परिवर्तन में, एक अटूट आशा जगती है,
और यही है हमारी मुक्ति का सच्चा सार।"

13. The Cascading Dreams

I stood on a rugged cliff,
Watching dreams cascade like a waterfall.
Each drop shimmered with pure ambition,
A vision of possibility falling freely,
Carrying the essence of my hidden hopes.

I remembered a time when I dared
To dream without limits or fear.
Every droplet seemed to echo
The fervour of my youthful aspirations,
Painting my world with vibrant hues.

As the water plunged into dark depths,
I felt the weight of reality below.
The cascade split into light and shadow,
Revealing a delicate balance
Between soaring hopes and grounded truths.

I walked closer to the edge,
Each step echoing inner uncertainty.
I watched the relentless flow of dreams
And wondered if my ambitions
Could withstand reality's pull.

In that moment, the waterfall of dreams
Became a mirror to my soul,
Reflecting both the thrill of ascent
And the risk of inevitable descent,
Teaching me that growth demands bold leaps.

I learned that every falling drop
Is both promise and sacrifice,
A silent call to rise again,
For embracing the fall is key
To forging lasting strength within.

I ventured along banks where water met stone,
Observing how each drop nurtured new life.
The cool mist revived my weary spirit,
Each ripple whispering secrets of renewal,
Reminding me that every descent holds rebirth.

In the end, the cascade of dreams became my guide,
An eternal beacon through both joy and despair.
My spirit soared with each echo of hope,
As the waterfall transformed me,
Lighting a path to future possibilities.

With every cascading drop, my heart found its rhythm,
Each ripple a gentle reminder of past ambitions.
The interplay of light and water bridged my memories,

Creating a harmonious blend of loss and renewal,
Fostering a quiet fire that urged me onward.

I embraced the surge of dreams as muse and mentor,
Letting each shimmering drop fuel a new resolve.
In the falling water, I rediscovered forgotten passions,
And the cascade became a silent pledge of possibility,
A promise that even the darkest falls birth fresh light.

"अब इस गिरती हुई आशाओं में,
हर बूंद में बसता है एक नया संकल्प,
जहाँ हर लहर सुनाती है,
उम्मीद और संकल्प की अनकही दास्ताँ।
इस प्रवाह में मिलती है, जीवन की नई सुबह का उजाला,
और हर पल में खुलता है, आत्मा का एक नया अरमान।"

14. The Wounded Bird

At dawn's earliest hush, I notice it there—
A small bird perched upon the windowsill.
Its wing hangs awkwardly, feathers ruffled by pain,
Yet an unspoken resolve dances in its eyes.
Outside, the sky warms to a soft pink glow,
Promising renewal even for a fragile spirit.

With every uncertain shuffle of its tiny feet,
I sense the echo of my own bruised stories.
Like that bird, I've known moments of fracture,
Where hope felt distant and breath laboured.
But here it sits, trembling yet steadfast,
Awaiting the first rays of a new beginning.

Sunlight spills across chipped paint and dusty glass,
Illuminating its silent vigil.
I wonder if the bird doubts the morning's promise,
Or if faith in tomorrow blooms instinctively in its heart.
Nature's resilience stands in quiet defiance,
Reminding me that even broken wings heal with time.

I recall my own seasons of darkness—
When each step felt like a leap over chasms of fear.
Yet somehow, dawn kept arriving,

A gentle tap on the soul, urging me to try again.
In the bird's patient gaze, I see a mirror
Reflecting all I once believed lost but found anew.

Day by day, as the sun journeys higher,
The bird attempts a careful stretch of its injured wing.
Feather by feather, the weight of despair lifts,
Replaced by a cautious whisper of flight.
In its steady recovery, I glean a lesson:
Healing is not sudden thunder; it is slow, certain light.

When at last it dares a flutter into the open air,
I feel a quiet rush of my own heart mending.
Its fragile departure is a simple declaration—
Scars don't nullify our capacity for flight;
They become the roadmap leading us
To new skies of possibility.

"एक टूटी हुई उम्मीद भी, भोर की किरणों से संवर सकती है,
जैसे उस घायल परिंदे ने पाया नए आसमान का रास्ता।
हर दर्द की लहर थमती नहीं, मगर कम ज़रूर हो जाती है,
और धीरे-धीरे, वही ज़ख़्म हमें उड़ने की वजह देते हैं—
क्योंकि हर टूटने में छुपी होती है एक नई उड़ान की कहानी।"

15. The Mending Heart

In a quiet room of solitude, a heart lay shattered,
Its pieces, scattered by the harsh winds of loss.
Once vibrant and whole, it now bore silent scars,
Every crack, a memory of love and despair.
The emptiness echoed with the pain of separation,
A fragile remnant of what once was.

Time, gentle and relentless, began to soothe the wounds,
Whispering soft lullabies of forgotten hope.
Each passing day offered a new touch of compassion,
A tender hand reaching out to mend what was broken.
The heart, though fragile, started to feel warmth anew,
A quiet promise that healing was on its way.

Slowly, the jagged edges softened under tender care,
As time wove its magic through every aching seam.
The scars, once symbols of painful loss,
Transformed into marks of resilience and strength.
Each line told a story of survival and courage,
A testament that beauty can arise from brokenness.

In the silence of recovery, the heart began to whisper,
Sharing secrets of vulnerability and hope.
It learned that exposure of its deepest wounds

Could be the very source of profound healing.
No longer did its fractures speak of weakness,
But of a power born from being truly seen.

Gentle echoes of empathy and kindness filled the space,
As loved ones and strangers alike offered their warmth.
Their compassion stitched together the frayed edges,
Creating a quilt of support around the wounded soul.
Every act of care was a quiet prayer of restoration,
A step toward embracing the imperfect self.

The mending heart began to beat with a new rhythm,
A pulse that sang of renewal and quiet strength.
It discovered that vulnerability was not a flaw,
But the doorway to a deeper, more authentic life.
The once-broken pieces now shone with their own light,
Illuminating a path paved by tender resilience.

In moments of reflection, the heart looked inward,
Seeing not only its past fractures but also its potential.
It embraced each scar as a mark of hard-won wisdom,
A reminder that every wound carried lessons of growth.
The journey of healing became a sacred pilgrimage,
A quest to honour the self in its raw, true form.

Days became months; the heart mended like a tapestry,
Woven with threads of sorrow, hope, and endless care.

The pain of yesterday softened into gentle recollection,
While new dreams began to kindle in the quiet light.
In that transformation, the heart found a resilient beauty,
A luminous beacon shining through its tender scars.

Now, the mending heart beats as a quiet testament,
A living story of overcoming and rebirth.
It serves as a guide for those still lost in darkness,
Showing that even shattered souls can be whole again.
Its light inspires others to embrace their vulnerabilities,
For in every broken piece lies the seed of new life.

"अब इस टूटे हुए दिल में,
नयी आशाओं का प्रबल प्रकाश जाग उठा है,
जहाँ हर निशाँ गवाही देता है,
कठिनाइयों से उपजी अटल शक्ति की।
यह दिल अब प्रेरणा का अमर स्रोत है,
जो हर दर्द को पुनरुत्थान के अग्नि में बदल देता है।"

16. The Chrysalis Dream

It began in a hush, between sleep and memory—
A velvety darkness cocooned me, gentle and terrifying.
I sensed my arms folded tight against my chest,
My breath slowed to a whisper,
As if all the world's noise had retreated
Into this womb of shifting shadows.

Colours pulsed just beyond the blackness—
Faint blues and dusky crimsons bleeding together.
They felt like echoes of my past,
Memories coiling around me as silky threads.
I tried to move but found my limbs bound
By a fragile barrier, a promise of metamorphosis.

In that otherworldly quiet, I heard my own heart:
A drumbeat calling from hidden chambers of the self.
With each pulse, the cocoon's film trembled,
Awakening a subtle friction—
It was equal parts fear and anticipation,
Like standing at the threshold of an undiscovered realm.

Gradually, the dream deepened,
And I glimpsed the silhouette of wings, half-formed.
Were they mine, or just a reflection

Of some longing I'd never voiced aloud?
I felt an urge to push, to tear, to break through,
As though my soul was straining for air.

A sudden rush of warmth rippled through the cocoon—
A surge of light that made the threads glimmer.
I pressed against them, testing the delicate barrier.
Tendrils of fear slithered in:
What if I emerge unfinished?
What if the world is not ready for me, nor I for it?

Then came the final snap of tension,
Threads unravelling under my gentle force.
I awoke, gasping, in a dawn-drenched room—
Skin tingling with the residue of silken webs,
A sense of newness pulsing through my veins.
The dream lingered, but so did a quiet conviction:
I had changed, and no one could undo it.

"जब नींद से उठकर मैंने अपना रूप टटोला,
अधूरी परतों के भीतर एक नया अस्तित्व चमक रहा था।
सवालों का शोर थमा, डर की परछाईं भी घुलने लगी—
क्योंकि उस रेशमी कैद से निकलकर
मैंने अपने भीतर एक नई उड़ान की आहट सुनी।
यही मेरा पुनर्जन्म है, यही मेरा नया सूरज।"

17. The Echoing Hall

I step into the marble vastness,
An abandoned throne room steeped in hush.
Columns soar to a vaulted sky,
Where chandeliers once dripped with splendour.
Now only shadows reside—
And an uncanny promise
That every word spoken here
Will resound a dozen times over.

I whisper, "I am not afraid,"
And the hall answers,
Not afraid... not afraid... not afraid...
Yet each echo strips another layer of truth,
As if asking: *Are you certain?*
A tremor races through my chest,
Betraying the fear
I swore I'd vanquish long ago.

I raise my voice: "I regret nothing,"
And it comes back louder, sharper:
Regret nothing... regret nothing... regret nothing...
But within that amplified chorus,
I hear an unspoken liar
Slice through the reverberations,

A phantom syllable revealing
Secrets I'd buried.

My footsteps carry me deeper,
Each echo a ghost of action—
A chance to undo, a chance to relive.
I sense old guilt trailing behind me,
Like a battered cape I cannot shed.
The Hall feels alive,
A keeper of confessions
That waits to be untangled.

Courage stirs in my lungs,
And I speak of love lost,
Of failings etched into memory—
"I wanted to stay, but..."
The Hall rises in reply:
Wanted to stay... wanted to stay... wanted to stay...
The resonance aches,
Bearing the heartbreak
I once tried to dismiss.

In the culminating hush,
I breathe out a single truth:
"I forgive myself."
An astonishing clarity rings back:
Forgive myself... forgive myself... forgive myself...

Their layered voices hold no blame now,
Only the promise
That acceptance can finally be heard.

Silence lingers a moment,
As though the Hall itself
Weighs my confession.
Then the echoes fade,
Leaving only my own steady pulse,
A quiet sign
That every echo,
In the end,
Is my voice returning home.

"इन दीवारों में दबे हैं
सच के अनगिनत प्रतिबिंब,
हर पुकार एक परछाईं
बनकर लौट आती है।
जब मैं ख़ुद को माफ़ करती हूँ,
ये गूँज भी नरम हो जाती है–
और अंदर कहीं
एक उजाले का दरवाज़ा खुल जाता है।"

18. The Unspoken Covenant

In a quiet moment beneath a twilight sky,
Two souls met in the gentle hum of destiny.
No words were spoken, only silent understanding,
A look shared, heavy with unspoken promises,
That spoke of a bond forged in vulnerability.

Their hearts, bruised by past sorrows, found solace,
In the tender space where empathy embraced them.
A silent pact formed without a single utterance,
A covenant sealed by the rhythm of shared pain,
And the delicate hope that tomorrow would be brighter.

In fleeting glances and soft smiles, they discovered
A resonance that transcended ordinary speech.
Each gesture was a pledge of trust and devotion,
An invisible thread weaving their lives together,
Binding them in a union of deep, heartfelt connection.

As days turned into nights, their bond grew stronger,
A guiding light amid life's unpredictable storms.
Through trials and triumphs, this silent promise endured,
A beacon that illuminated even the darkest paths,
Encouraging them to move forward with firm faith.

In moments of quiet reflection, they recalled
The power of that unspoken understanding,
The warmth of shared tears and silent laughter,
That nurtured a connection beyond simple words,
An eternal covenant etched in the depths of their souls.

They travelled separate roads yet moved as one,
Each step fortified by the strength of their bond.
Even in solitude, the memory of that pact
Served as a soft whisper in the heart,
Guiding them through both hardships and celebrations.

Their unspoken covenant became a sanctuary,
A quiet refuge where honesty and vulnerability met.
In the stillness of life's many challenges,
They found courage in the echo of shared dreams,
A luminous thread that wove hope into every day.

"अब इस मौन समझौते में,
हर दिल में दमकता है अटूट, प्रबल विश्वास,
जहाँ मौन में ही संलग्न होता है गहरा, अटल प्रेम,
हर पल झिलमिलाती है नई, उज्जवल ऊर्जा,
और आत्मा में गूंजती है – यही है असली, अनंत दास्ताँ।"

19. The Crimson Tide

A blood-red surge roars along a barren shoreline,
Waves of fervour smash against jagged cliffs.
The horizon glows with a raw, untamed fire,
Each swell echoes burning desire
And quiet sorrow in every crashing wave.

This tide, hued in deep crimson and melancholy,
Sweeps away remnants of old heartaches
With relentless force and quiet persistence.
It leaves behind shattered dreams and fragile hopes,
A tempestuous dance of wild passion
Mingled with tender, yearning whispers.

Beneath its surging surface, turbulent emotions churn,
Fierce passion mingles with the bitter taste of regret.
The rhythm of the storm beats like aching heartbeats,
Each wave recalls tender moments turned to ash,
Yet hints at the soft spark of healing light
Waiting to emerge from the depths.

The relentless tide is both destructive and cleansing,
Washing away remnants of past wounds
In its fierce, all-encompassing embrace.
It challenges the soul to plunge into raw emotion,

Inviting one to rebuild and be reborn
Amidst the chaos of the swirling sea.

Navigating this scarlet surge demands a fearless heart,
One must ride the crest of passion
While taming despair's relentless undertow.
Every step on wet, red sand is a battle
And a blessing—a reminder that vulnerability
Is both the seed and the harvest of change.

In the echo of crashing waves, a silent testament unfolds,
A story written in tears and fervent dreams.
The ocean's roar speaks of a soul that has loved fiercely,
Yet in its eternal cycle lies the promise
Of renewal—a chance to rise anew from the ashes.

"अब इस रक्तिम तरंग में छुपी है एक अनकही प्रेम कथा,
जहाँ हर लहर में मिलता है टूटे दिल का एक नया इशारा।
हर तरंग में बसी है दर्द की भी एक मीठी कहानी,
और इस अशांत समंदर में खिलता है नया सवेरा का उजाला।
हर गूंज में सुनाई देती है पुनरुत्थान की पुकार,
और हर अंधेरी लहर में बसता है सच्चा, मधुर प्रेम का एहसास।"

20. The Phoenix's Feather

A single crimson feather lay on the ash-strewn path,
Glinting under a tired sun.
It called to anyone with a history of mistakes,
A magnet for every scar, every regret.
Even at first glance, something about its glow
Whispered both ruin and rebirth.

He reached for it with trembling curiosity,
Fingertips brushing its strange radiance.
In that instant, illusions burst forth—
Old failures reeled across his vision:
A friendship shattered by pride,
A promise broken in a careless moment.

These spectres loomed real enough to wound,
Crashing over him like a wave of memory.
His breath caught in his throat,
Ash swirling around his ankles.
The feather flickered, stoking the furnace
Of every heartbreak he thought buried.

A voice echoed in the hush:
Embrace the burn; let pain be the tinder.
Flames licked at the edges of his regrets,

Turning them from raw sorrow
Into glowing embers of understanding.
In their light, he saw possibility flicker.

The illusions, once suffocating in darkness,
Now shimmered with a strange beauty.
For in each failure lay a lesson,
A path untaken waiting to be forged anew.
He felt the feather's heat intensify—
Not destructive, but purifying.

The moment the final failure evaporated,
A silent explosion of ash filled the air,
Yet the feather remained, blazing with life.
He clutched it close, heart pounding.
Here was proof that from the ashes
One could rise, soul scorched clean of yesterdays.

"भय और पश्चाताप की राख में
छुपा है एक अग्नि का बीज,
जो हर टूटन को नई उड़ान देता है।
जब फ़ीनिक्स के पर की आँच ने
पुराने ज़ख़्मों को मिटा डाला,
तभी भीतर का सूरज
फिर से चमक उठा—
एक नया आरंभ, एक नई शुरुआत।"

21. The Glass Bridge

High above a canyon's gaping mouth,
A bridge of glass shimmers against the horizon.
Daylight spills through every transparent plank,
Making each step feel like walking on fragile air.
The wind howls with a strange melody—
A warning, or an invitation?

Below lies a sea of mist, swirling in silent threat,
As if it yearns to swallow any trembling soul.
My heart thunders like a warning drum,
Wary of each creak and distant echo.
Yet a voice inside whispers:
To move forward is to trust what you cannot see.

Inches turn to feet, feet into daring strides,
And clarity cuts through me like cold glass.
I witness every hairline fracture beneath my shoes,
Reflecting my doubts, my insecurities.
Some part of me wants to retreat,
But the weight of possibility pulls me onward.

Fear's sharp edge glistens in the crystal floor—
A reflection of the self I've tried to hide.
One misstep could send me plummeting,

Yet staying still is no less perilous.
The horizon is a promise of something new,
Though it stands behind a gauntlet of my own design.

A gust of wind rattles the structure,
And I cling to the railing, breath catching in my throat.
This is the moment where illusions die—
Where I learn if my courage is more than a fleeting wish.
The glass beneath me seems to whisper truths
I've kept buried beneath routine and fear.

Steadfast, I look ahead at a future unknown,
A future shaped by the honesty of each step.
I realize clarity is not gentle;
It's as ruthless as it is pure.
But liberation demands that I face my reflections
Without flinching from the fractures that define me.

"नज़र उठती है उस पार, जहाँ धुंध में छुपा है नया सफ़र,
काँच के हर टुकड़े में झलकती है मेरी दुविधा और हौसला।
डर के हर कंपन को पार करके ही, मैं अपनी मंज़िल देख पाऊँगी—
क्योंकि पारदर्शी राह में ही छिपा है,
एक सच्चा अक्स मेरी पहचान का।"

22. The Veil of Illusion

A mysterious veil drifts
Between shadow and light,
Where reality mingles
With whispered dreams.
It shimmers softly along
The border of truth and fantasy,
A silent barrier dividing
What is real from imagined.

A lone seeker stands
Before this drifting curtain,
Reaching out with trembling hands
To pull it aside.
Curiosity and caution merge
In every deliberate gesture,
As they prepare to unveil
Secrets hidden behind the guise.

With each gentle tug,
The fragile boundary trembles,
Truth and deception blur
Within its wavering fabric.
The veil quivers under
The weight of a questioning heart,

Revealing secrets that dance
Between illusion and fact.

In that suspended moment,
The seeker pauses in uncertainty,
Wondering if these visions
Are comforting dreams or confining lies.
Every flicker of light offers
Solace mixed with a whisper of doubt,
Inviting the mind to wander
Through realms of uncertain wonder.

In this fragile twilight of revelation,
The seeker catches a fleeting reflection,
A mirror of hidden desires
And quietly stirring fears.
Each thought is bathed in soft glow,
Drawing them deeper into self-discovery.

The interplay of reality and perception
Becomes a silent dialogue,
Where each illusion challenges
The soul to look deeper.
In this delicate tension,
Comfort and confinement intertwine,
Forcing one to reconsider
What has long been taken for granted.

Slowly, the veil unveils its hidden mosaic
Of truth and artifice,
Each shimmering thread carrying
Echoes of both hope and despair.
The seeker finds that the line
Between dream and reality fades,
A delicate balance that liberates
And binds the spirit.

In the quiet aftermath, clarity dawns
Like the first light of day,
Teaching the seeker that every illusion
Holds its own bittersweet grace.
They learn to embrace mystery,
Life's eternal blend of light and shadow,
Discovering deeper truths
Through the art of thoughtful questioning.

"अब इस परदे के पीछे छुपा है
सच्चाई और माया का संगम,
जहाँ हर झलक में मिलता है
अनदेखी राहों का संदेश।
इस रहस्यमय पर्दे को अपनाते हुए,
मिलता है उजाला,
और हर सवाल में उभरता है
जीवन का गहरा, मधुर सार।"

23. The Puppeteer's Strings

Under the hush of dim theatre lights,
He grips the wooden crossbars in both hands—
Threads cascading like lifelines
That links him to painted marionettes.
Their carved eyes remain vacant,
Awaiting his silent command.

The audience buzzes with hushed anticipation,
Drawn to the stage's mystique.
At the slightest twitch of his finger,
The puppets bow in choreographed grace,
Their limbs dancing through tragedies
He orchestrated for their wooden world.

As the act unfolds,
He feels a peculiar pull on his shoulders,
Subtle yet undeniable.
A quiver rattles his composure—
Could another force control him too?
A fleeting dread creeps into his steady gaze.

Between scenes, he packs away each puppet,
Folding their limbs in padded cases.
Yet standing among the dusty curtains,

He feels a nameless heaviness.
Their blank stares reflect something essential—
A mirror of the roles he thought were entirely his.

Night after night, he returns to the stage,
The same illusions enchanting the crowd.
Still, every pull of the string reverberates within him,
As if an ancient chorus whispers:
"Control is but a phantom—
And all of us perform within its grasp."

One fateful evening, alone in the wings,
He sees threads descending from the rafters,
Tied to his trembling shoulders.
A thunderclap of awareness strikes,
Revealing him as but a puppet,
Tethered to an unseen will.

"उन कठपुतलियों के नर्तन के बीच
वह अपनी छाया खोजता रहा,
डोरियाँ जो उसकी मुट्ठी में थीं,
वो दरअसल उसे भी थामे हुई थीं।
इसी रहस्य ने उसकी आँखें खोल दीं—
कभी-कभी हम सब
अदृश्य हाथों की चाल में बँधे होते हैं,
यही सोच का छलावा
हमारे होने को परिभाषित करता है।"

24. The Voice Behind the Wall

He steps into a corridor of endless dusk,
Its walls soaring on either side like silent monoliths.
Patches of moss cling to stone slabs,
And the floor is slick with condensation.
A lone lantern in his hand casts jittery shadows,
Revealing how narrow his path truly is.

At the very first turn, he hears it:
A hushed murmur behind the nearest wall—
Soft, trembling, strangely familiar.
He presses a cautious ear to the cold surface,
Senses a child's laughter woven with quiet sobs.
The sound tugs at him, unearthing a half-buried ache
He never realized he still carried.

Further on, the corridor widens,
Yet the darkness feels heavier,
As though the stone passages cradle secrets
Waiting to be unearthed.
Behind a second wall, a voice rasps accusations,
Each syllable laced with shame.
A chill rushes along his spine—
He recognizes its timbre from long nights of regret.

He moves deeper into the labyrinth,
Lantern light dancing off chipped bricks.
Echoes rise from unseen recesses:
Fragments of confession, muted sobs,
Moments of joy twisted by remorse.
It dawns on him that every voice,
However distinct, belongs to a single source—
And that source is intimately tied to his own past.

Water drips from a crack overhead,
A steady, mournful tap echoing in the gloom.
The path forks, each passage whispering different names,
As though summoning him to face
Forgotten versions of himself.
He glances down at his trembling hands
And wonders when he last truly listened
To the quiet corners of his own mind.

Rounding a final bend, he encounters
A broad chamber where the walls converge.
A chorus of voices blooms from every side—
Childhood dreams, suppressed fury,
Sweet promises never kept.
They swirl around him in a symphony of longing,
Each clamour for acknowledgement
Demanding he claim them as his own.

Sinking to his knees, he lets the lantern fall,
Its flame casting a restless glow upon stone.
In that vulnerable moment, he comprehends
That only by embracing these hidden echoes
Can he become whole.
Beneath the rising tide of voices,
He whispers a vow of acceptance,
A gentle promise to bring them into the light.

"इन भटकती आवाज़ों में
वो अपने ही सुरों का प्रतिबिंब पाता है।
हर इल्तिजा, हर शिकायत
कभी अनसुनी रह गई थी।
इस स्याह गलियारे के अंत में
उसने अपनी ही आहट पहचानी—
और उसी पहचान ने
उसे मुकम्मल बना दिया।"

25. The Gravity of Silence

They arrived from far corners of everyday life,
Some drawn by a deep faith that a few hours of silence
Could unravel a quieter kind of transformation,
Others merely curious—perhaps even skeptical—
About how the absence of speech
Might soften minds steeped in the churn of noise.
Yet they gathered all the same, brimming with questions,
Carrying uncertain hopes in weary hearts—
Ready to test their resolve against an echoing void
Where words would not be heard.

Within that hush, the hall stands crowded,
Each voice locked behind still lips.
Footsteps echo faintly, forming a subtle language
Of caution, awe, and intent.
Moonlight spills in diagonal beams,
Silvering the quiet like an invisible curtain
Draped across every face.
A quiet unity resonates in every silent gaze.
In this suspended realm, they sense
An odd liberation in the very act of not speaking,
As though a chorus of truths might finally
Find the space to breathe.

Silent tension trembles between those gathered,
Eyes flickering with unvoiced stories.
A tear glides down one cheek, acknowledged by a nod,
No syllable to soften its impact,
Only compassion shaped by small gestures.
Another pair shares a fleeting smile,
Unsure if relief or longing drives it,
Yet trusting that in this hush,
A bond can forge without a single word.

A coin slips from someone's grasp,
Striking marble with a sudden metallic ring.
It startles them all,
Like a lone bell in a deserted valley.
Briefly, glances converge,
And in that swift communion of silence,
They realize how a single sound
Can become the voice they've hesitated to release.
In that echo, hearts find courage to speak in whispers,
As silence weaves solace into each trembling breath.

Dawn nudges the windowpanes,
Its warmth dissolving the moon's pale sheen.
Still, no one breaks the unspoken pact.
In the hush, illusions crack,
Truths rise, acceptance dawns.
They sense a gentle parting of the heart's armour,

As though every silent story is finally heard—
Proof that words, though precious,
Are sometimes too frail
To carry the full weight of what we yearn to share.

"खामोशी की इस भीड़ में,
हर शब्द में एक छुपी हुई आग जलती है,
बिन बोले, हर धड़कन में दर्द और आशा गूँजती है।
सुबह की पहली किरण, जैसे किसी प्राचीन रहस्य की अनुगूँज,
हर मन के जख्मों पर नई रोशनी बिखेरती है—
इस मौन में, हर कहानी अपनी पीड़ा और जीत कहती है,
और अंत में, एक नया उदय हमें स्वयं से मिलाता है।"

26. The Celestial Mantle

A shimmering mantle unfurls
Across the obsidian night.
It drapes like a silken curtain
Over the cosmos' secret stage.
Its delicate folds obscure
The edges of what we know.

Guarding ancient truths
With a mystic, timeless allure,
The universe whispers enigmas
Through a gentle, hazy glow.
It invites the curious
To pause and ponder mysteries.

A lone wanderer stands
Beneath this vast, starlit canopy,
Eyes lifted toward the glowing mantle
Which parts the infinite with quiet grace.
In that silent moment,
Cosmos reveals grandeur and intimacy.

Every ripple of light
Murmurs forgotten legends
Of celestial lore.

The air vibrates softly,
Inviting meditation
On unseen, potent forces.

As the mantle dances with the night,
It weaves dreams and memories—
An interplay of destiny and desire.
Its shimmer hints at secrets
Cradled deep in cosmic depths,
Each star a beacon of quiet wisdom.

It blurs the boundary
Between the known and the unfathomable,
Leaving one to wonder
At the silent mysteries that bind us.
A tender enigma beckons
The soul to dream beyond limits.

Peering through the translucent dark,
The wanderer sees not just distant galaxies,
But fragments of an inner universe—
A mirror of hidden emotions
And subtle personal epiphanies,
Where the expansive and intimate entwine.

The celestial mantle is both
A barrier and a bridge,

Separating the outer realm
From the inner sanctum of being.
Through its ephemeral shimmer,
Truth seeps gently into the heart.

It invites exploration
Of the delicate dance between destiny and desire,
Revealing that life's deepest truths
Lie shrouded in mystery.
Every quiet pulse of light
Guides the soul like a soft beacon.

Stars whisper secrets in the silent night,
Each twinkle reveals infinite hope's promise,
The cosmic canvas unveils hidden truths,
Mysteries echo softly in the endless void,
Every pulse inspires a dawn of dreams,
Lighting paths to a soulful awakening.

"अब इस आकाशगंगा की चादर में,
छुपा है रहस्यों का असीम संसार,
जहाँ हर चमकता तारा सुनाता है
एक अनकही दास्ताँ, गहरी अनसुलझी सच्चाई,
इस चादर के पीछे बसी है
आत्मा की अनदेखी, रहस्यमय परतों के राज़।"

27. The Forgotten Sonata

In a grand, abandoned hall,
Echoes once filled the air.
Dust dances in fractured moonlight,
Whispering of a lost era.
A ghostly sonata lingers,
Like a wistful memory revived.
Its haunting melody drifts,
Softly through the heavy silence.

A tune of passion and loss
Weaves through every note.
It whispers stories of days
When music stirred eager souls.
Every chord once brought life,
Infusing still air with vibrance.
Hearts moved in perfect rhythm,
To the pulse of joyous applause.

Now, empty corridors cradle remnants
Of that vibrant, fading tune.
Faint notes bear untold dreams,
Echoing bittersweet, faded memories.
They call out to hearts,
Yearning for lost, timeless beauty.

Each note speaks a longing,
Both tender and resolute.
The sonata's melody drifts
Like a spectral sigh across the room.
Each chord paints a delicate stroke
On time's expansive, silent canvas.
It conjures images of graceful dancers,
Of tender, fleeting love affairs.
Moments, fragile yet eternal,
Intertwine with each gentle refrain.

The music speaks in a language
Of deep longing and quiet resolve.
A soft reminder that beauty
Is never entirely lost.
It lives in the echo
Of a once-radiant refrain.
Awaiting rediscovery by a soul
Willing to truly listen.
Every reverberation calls to awaken
Forgotten dreams from slumber.
It bridges the present and a distant past,
Stirring embers of passion within.
Desolation transforms into hope
And renewal through its soft strains.
It invites one to reclaim
Lost fragments of the soul.

Allowing music to heal old scars,
Each note becomes a tender salve.
Restoring wonder and possibility,
Breathing life into faded dreams.
The hall, steeped in memory, listens
With quiet, enduring grace.
As the ghostly sonata weaves
A tapestry of heartache and delight.
Every lingering note promises
That time cannot erase its magic.
Its harmonies pulse like a heartbeat,
Echoing eternal, unyielding longing.

In quiet corners of this forgotten place,
Silence itself hums a soft refrain.
A melody once lit the darkest nights,
Imbuing the air with bygone magic.
The forgotten sonata beckons,
With soulful, magnetic allure.
Each note gently reminds us
Of life's ephemeral, splendid beauty.

It urges you to pause,
To listen deeply to your inner song.
Recalling dreams that once set your spirit ablaze,
Rekindling hope in every whisper.

In its tender, haunting strains,
An unspoken truth emerges:
Even in decay, beauty endures,
And hope forever sings.

"अब इस वीरान हॉल में,
हर सुर गूँजता है अनकही दास्ताँ,
जहाँ हर धुन में छुपा है
खोए प्रेम और पुरानी उम्मीद का सार।
इस साज की मधुरता में बसते हैं,
दिल के अनगिनत राज़,
जो सुनने वाले को बुलाते हैं,
फिर से जगाने को उस खोई ख़ुशी की बयार।
हर धड़कन में मिलती है,
संगीत की एक नई कहानी,
और हर लय में गूँजता है,
जीवन का अनंत, मधुर एहसास।"

28. The Silent Carnival

In the heart of a deserted carnival,
Faded lights barely flicker in silence.
Empty rides and vacant booths stand,
Echoing memories of joyful laughter,
Now lost to the passage of time.

Once, the carnival burst with vibrant colour,
Masks adorned faces in festive glee,
Music and laughter filled the air,
A dance of life and celebration,
Now only echoes remain in the dark.

Behind each empty booth, a secret whispers,
Tales of masked performances and hidden sorrows,
Where smiles concealed unspoken despair,
And every facade guarded a private pain,
Layered deep beneath public gaiety.

In this quiet decay, the carnival becomes a mirror,
Reflecting the interplay of light and shadow,
Of authentic hearts versus crafted performances,
Where outward joy hides inner melancholy,
And each vacant seat cradles an untold story.

Masked celebrations once ignited hope and wonder,
Yet now silence reveals a lonely truth,
For lives wear facades to charm the world,
While secret tears fall behind closed eyes,
Exposing the bittersweet nature of existence.

The silent carnival calls for introspection,
A gentle invitation to strip away pretense,
To uncover the genuine self beneath the mask,
And embrace the raw beauty of vulnerability,
Finding joy in truth rather than in illusion.

Within this abandoned ground, a tender promise lingers,
That hidden joy can be rediscovered in honesty,
Where private sorrows meet the light of renewal,
Transforming despair into a quiet, resilient hope,
And every silent corner holds a spark of life.

"अब इस सुनसान मेला में,
हर साया छुपाता है अनकही पीड़ा,
जहाँ चेहरे पर मुस्कान छुपाती है दर्द,
हर कोने में बसी है एक अनकही कहानी,
जो दिल को गहराई से छू जाती है,
और हर मौन में सुनाई देती है सच्ची राहत।"

29. The Forgotten Temple

Long ago, this courtyard thrummed with hymns,
Torches casting dancing shadows on carved pillars.
Now, in the hush of midnight's breath,
A chill wind sweeps fallen leaves across cracked marble.
Stillness hangs, as though mourning an abandoned faith.

I wander through arched doorways, silent as ghosts,
Tracing fingertips over faded murals of gods and saints.
Each image seems to echo with lost devotion,
Stories that once guided trembling hearts
Now flake away under the moon's pale stare.

High above, a broken spire juts into the star-flecked sky,
Its gilded tip long since stolen by looters or time.
I sense the echo of ancient prayers drifting in the rafters,
Soft as a sigh, persistent as a memory,
Yearning for an ear willing to listen.

Grains of dust swirl under torchlight remnants,
Each speck a story of belief worn thin.
Could these stones still hold a heartbeat of faith,
Or does emptiness reign where once light burned bright?
I feel the night's silence beckon me deeper,
Tempting me to pry open the layers of lost devotion.

Perhaps faith never perished here;
It only retreated beneath the rubble,
Waiting for a gentle touch, a renewed vow.
A flicker of hope kindles in my chest—
That in this vast darkness, the smallest glow
Might still awaken a song once thought forever lost.

In the temple's innermost chamber, I pause—
The air is thick with centuries of secrets.
My heartbeat resonates against the cold stone floors,
Matching a rhythm older than words.
I realize that absence itself can be a prayer,
A quiet vigil holding space for rebirth.

"इस उजड़े मंदिर की दरारों में, अब भी कुछ सुर बचे हैं,
सदियों के सन्नाटे में गूँजती है एक अनसुनी पुकार।
शायद आस्था कभी मरती नहीं, वो बस ख़ामोशी में पलती है—
और जब कोई दिल इसका एहसास करने आता है,
वही विरानगी एक नए विश्वास की नींव रख जाती है।"

30. The Garden of Echoes

In a hidden garden where twilight softly reigns,
Every flower hums with the voices of days past.
Petals shimmer with echoes of forgotten laughter,
Their fragrances carry whispers of bygone memories.
Each bloom stands as a testament to moments lost,
A secret haven where the past gently lingers,
And in the quiet glow, time itself seems to sigh.

Strolling along winding paths, the protagonist listens,
Hearing soft murmurs woven into the rustle of leaves.
Every blossom tells a story of joy and sorrow,
Reawakening long-forgotten moments with each breath.
The garden becomes an archive of cherished memories,
Where the air holds both regret and sweet reminiscence,
As the gentle symphony of nature cradles their soul.

Amid the living echoes, the wanderer finds solace,
Each step stirs a cascade of recollections and dreams.
The gentle hum of each flower invites reflection,
Unfolding layers of emotion like petals in bloom.
A quiet dialogue emerges between memory and now,
Reviving the spirit with each tender, whispered note,
In this soft embrace, the heart learns to listen anew.

Within this sanctuary, beauty and melancholy entwine,
The harsh notes of loss blend with soft strains of hope.
Every wilted petal and vibrant bloom shares its secret,
A reminder that growth often springs from tender scars.
The garden nurtures the soul by embracing both pain
And grace in the fleeting moments of time,
Here, every breath is a silent hymn to resilience.

Amid these living echoes, transformation takes root,
As each fragile flower reveals its quiet resilience.
New shoots push through old, withering memories,
Merging past with the promise of renewal.
This gentle metamorphosis whispers of rebirth,
Inviting the wanderer to embrace change with heart,
In each emerging bud, hope unfurls like a promise.

Healing blossoms in the interplay of bitter and sweet,
The protagonist learns to tend every fragile memory,
Nurturing both shadows and the light of past days,
Each recollection becoming a stepping stone to growth.
The garden's living echoes offer solace and guidance,
A call to transform grief into the art of moving forward,
Every tender moment becomes a seed for tomorrow.

As time flows through this grove, the soul is reborn,
Memories shape a resilient self with each passing hour.
Every fragrant whisper is a promise of renewal,

A tender invitation to release what was once lost,
Embracing the evolving beauty of life's tapestry,
Where healing is found in every living echo,
And beneath the boughs, destiny sings a new beginning.

"अब इस गुप्त बगिया में,
हर फूल में छुपा है एक नया संदेश,
जहाँ हर सुगंध बताती है,
बीते कल की यादों का अनमोल सार।
हर पंखुड़ी में मिलता है,
दर्द और खुशी का संगम,
जो हमें सिखाता है,
कि हर क्षण में छुपा है नवजीवन का उजाला।
यह बगिया है आत्मा की सच्ची दास्ताँ,
जहाँ हर गूँज में मिलती है,
पुनरुत्थान की मधुर कहानी।"

31. The Mystic Maze

Under a starlit sky,
A traveller enters a labyrinth,
Where walls twist and shift
In a playful dance of light.
Every corridor shimmers
With vibrant hues of possibility,
Inviting the wanderer into
A realm of endless wonder—
A space where mystery unfolds
With each curious step.
Every turn whispers secrets unknown.

The maze reveals not sorrow,
But echoes of joy untold.
Beams of magical radiance
Paint murals of hope on stone,
While laughter and song
Linger like soft, hidden melodies.
Ancient inscriptions murmur
Tales of vibrant beginnings,
Each turn igniting
A vision of life's bright future.
Every passage renews
The spirit with its silent promise.

Along winding paths,
The traveller discovers secret gardens,
Bursting with luminescent blossoms
And streams that shimmer in the dusk.
In this enchanted space,
Whispers of the earth rise gently—
Each petal and ripple
Reminds one of nature's endless creativity,
A quiet invitation
To embrace the beauty of now.
A hidden fragrance of renewal fills the air.

Mystical creatures appear,
Dancing lightly through the maze,
Their presence a joyful echo
Of worlds beyond our knowing.
They guide with radiant smiles,
Sharing secrets of inner strength
And limitless possibility,
Casting soft light on the journey,
A glow that warms the wandering soul.
Their silent footsteps trace paths of ancient lore.

Every step becomes
A celebration of self-discovery,
As the labyrinth transforms

Into a vibrant tapestry of dreams.
The traveller learns
This maze is not a trap but a portal,
Opening hearts to moments of pure magic,
Where wonder blossoms
At every unexpected twist.
A surge of delight
Accompanies each forward stride.

In a hidden courtyard,
Nature's symphony fills the air—
Ancient vines and murmuring streams
Weave a song of renewal.
The gentle whisper of the wind
Carries memories of forgotten days,
A chorus of nature celebrating
Each leaf and blossom,
A serene interlude amid the maze's pulse.
Every note of nature sings a lullaby of rebirth.

The labyrinth mirrors
The traveller's inner light,
Reflecting hopes, dreams,
And vivid visions of tomorrow.
No longer shadowed by the past,
Every stride sings of rebirth;
Each corridor opens a fresh chapter

Of discovery and delight,
A journey where every heartbeat
Resounds with endless energy.
This inner echo transforms
The path into a mosaic of life.

As the maze widens
Into a vast, luminous expanse,
The traveller stands awestruck
By the promise of boundless possibility.
Shifting walls become a canvas
Brushed with streaks of radiant light,
Each ray a gentle vow
Of growth, renewal,
And quiet transformation.
In that open vastness, dreams take flight.

"अब इस जादुई भूलभुलैया में,
हर मोड़ पर खिलती है आशा की किरण,
जहाँ हर दीवार अपनी कहानी गाती है,
और हर कदम में छुपा है जीवन का रंग,
यहाँ हर दिल में बसती है अनंत उमंग,
जो हर पल में भर देती है नई ऊर्जा,
और हमें याद दिलाती है कि हमारी आत्मा
में छुपी है असीम शक्ति और उजाला,
जो निरंतर हमे आगे बढ़ने का संदेश देती है,
और हर सांस में नयी उम्मीद का प्रकाश जगमगाता है।"

32. The Stilled Clock

At the centre of the bustling town
Stood a proud clock tower, tall and resolute.
Its chimes had long governed daily rhythms—
Morning wake-ups, hurried lunches, dusk gatherings.
Yet one silent moment revealed a secret pause.
And then, one dawn, the hands froze in place,
And silence claimed the tick-tock heartbeat.

Time itself seemed to pause,
As if the universe held its breath.
The cosmos waited in hushed anticipation.
A ripple of wonder stirred the air,
Whispering secrets of moments unclaimed.
The halted hands mirrored our silent hearts,
Each second suspended in tender mystery.

People stopped in mid-step, glancing upward,
Wondering if the gears inside had finally broken.
Businessmen paused their rushed commutes,
Children stared wide-eyed, unsure if classes start.
A quiet awe spread through the crowd.
For a moment, traffic hissed to a hush,
As though the entire town held its breath.

Curiosity replaced routine; eyes lingered on stillness.
Without the clock's relentless urging,
Cafés brimmed with unhurried conversations,
Artists sketched daydreams on café napkins,
And neighbours had more than a nod to share.
The silence wove a tapestry of renewed connections.
Time's tyranny seemed suspended in graceful pause.

In cozy attics and cramped offices,
Hearts dared to revisit dusty aspirations.
One woman found her journal of half-forgotten poems,
A man rediscovered his old guitar.
Freed from clock-bound obligations,
They pursued passions that had long been muted
By the relentless race of hours.

The marketplace hummed differently—
Merchants chatted amiably with customers,
No one glancing at a watch,
No horns blaring for someone to hurry along.
A gentle wonder swept through the lanes,
As if life's soundtrack had slowed to a mindful melody.
Every vendor and passerby embraced this pause.

Yet a tinge of unease mingled with the newfound calm.
Without time's structure, some felt adrift,
Shaken by the quiet revelation:

How much of living had they neglected
In the name of punctuality and progress?
A collective sigh whispered of reclaimed time.
They began to question the cost of each second.

After two days, the clock's gears whirred back to life,
Its hands resuming their measured march.
But something in the townspeople had shifted—
They carried a quieter wisdom, a gentler pace.
Now they knew: a moment's stillness
Could birth entire worlds of possibility.

"जब उस घड़ी ने अपनी चाल रोकी,
शहर में ठहर गई एक अनकही ख़ामोशी;
रफ़्तार थम गई, जैसे हर पल में गहराई बस गई;
घटों में उम्मीदों की धीमी धड़कनें गूंजने लगीं;
हर मोड़ पर नए अरमान उभरते रहे;
हर साँस में जीवन की नयी राह झलकती रही;
यह ठहराव बन गया आत्म-विश्लेषण का दर्पण;
और फिर, समय ने एक नए सुकून के साथ दस्तक दी,
जिसमें हर क्षण ने एक नवीन शुरुआत का आह्वान किया।"

33. The River of Remorse

On a moonlit night, I found the river,
Its surface glimmering with ghostly light.
Legends spoke of its waters carrying sorrows
Far from the weary soul.
Yet approaching its bank, I felt a quiver of doubt—
Am I ready to let go of what's weighed me down?

A hush lingered above the current,
As if the very air dared not disturb
The silent confessions it bore.
I knelt at the edge, saw my reflection
Waver in the dark ripples,
My face rippling with every unspoken regret.

Shards of memory floated past—
A carelessly spoken word,
A promise broken out of negligence,
An apology never uttered.
They shimmered under the moon's watchful gaze,
Beckoning me to confront them at last.

With trembling courage, I dipped my hand in,
Feeling the chill seep through my bones.
At once, the river seemed to whisper

Names, moments, half-forgotten dreams.
A mosaic of guilt and yearning
Pressed against my heart.

I stepped forward, water rising to my waist,
Each regret tugging at my skin
Like ghosts craving attention.
It hurt to acknowledge
The depths of my own failings—
Yet strangely, the deeper I waded, the lighter I felt.

In that flowing current, I sensed a choice:
Either cling to remorse as a familiar burden
Or let the water cleanse each wound.
But letting go meant vulnerability,
Surrendering pride and self-reproach,
Trusting that mistakes can be footprints toward growth.

Then, as if answering my unspoken plea,
The river's current turned gentle,
Carrying fragments of shame away.
What remained was a hush—
A space to forgive myself and understand
My imperfections in a fragile, human tapestry.

With the moon sinking low, I emerged,
Water dripping like fresh tears.

No thunder heralded my release,
No chorus of angels graced the night,
Only a soft, abiding peace remained,
As the river transmuted remorse to quiet acceptance.

"उस बहती धारा में मैंने अपने अपराधों को बहा दिया,
हर बूँद ले गई एक-एक बोझ को कुछ दूर आगे।
अधूरी माफ़ी और झूठी दलीलों से आज़ाद होकर,
मैंने पहली बार हल्केपन का एहसास किया–
मानो उसी पवित्र जल में,
मैंने खुद को एक नए रंग में ढाल लिया।"

34. The Candle in the Catacombs

She stepped carefully into the cold passage,
Each footfall echoing along the ancient stone.
A candle flickered in her grasp, fragile yet steadfast,
Its small glow challenging the vast darkness.
Shadows danced upon the walls,
As though the catacombs themselves watched, waiting.

With every turn, the corridors revealed new depths—
Bone-littered corners and motifs of forgotten faith.
The tiny flame seemed almost out of place
In such an ocean of night,
But it guided her nonetheless,
A silent companion in a silent realm.

She paused at a branching path,
Unsure of where the deeper hollows led.
A breath caught in her throat,
Memories tugging her thoughts toward fear.
Yet the candle's gentle sway spoke reassurance,
Promising that a single light could banish gloom.

Every step echoed a ghostly hymn,
Whispers of forgotten souls flitted in the dark,

Ancient secrets murmured through stone arches,
The candle's glow revealed relics of lost eras,
Time itself seemed suspended in silent reverence,
A fragile hope stirred within the cold gloom.

Shadows and light danced a quiet duet,
Tracing memories along weathered walls,
Every flicker wrote a story of despair and grace,
While the damp air carried echoes of lost chants,
The night bore witness to secrets whispered low,
Binding heart and stone in a moment of solemn awe,
And in that hushed silence, hope stirred softly anew.

Water dripped in distant chambers,
A metronome of unease echoing through the vaults.
The candle sputtered but refused to die,
Its glow casting fleeting silhouettes
That turned monstrous shapes into mere illusions.
She steadied her pulse, determined to press on.

In the labyrinth's farthest chamber,
Where the air seemed thick with centuries of quiet,
She felt a surge of vulnerability,
As though the walls whispered ancient regrets.
Yet the candle's warm halo persisted,
Proof that, in darkness, hope emerges brightest.

Eventually, she glimpsed a faint gleam ahead—
A promise of morning's arrival through a hidden shaft.
The candle fluttered, merging with the new light,
As though handing its duty over to the dawn.
In that confluence of shadows and sunrise,
She realized a powerful truth:
Even the tiniest flame lights up an entire world of doubt.

"अँधेरे तहख़ानों में भी
ये नन्ही लौ अडिग रही।
दीवारों पर सरकता सन्नाटा
हर साँस में ख़ौफ़ जगाता रहा—
पर उस उजाले की कोमल गरमी
आस की नई राह बनाती गई।
जब भोर की पहली किरण ने दस्तक दी,
तम को हराने के लिए
एक छोटी रौशनी ही काफ़ी निकली।"

35. The Radiant Abyss

In the depths of a shadowed chasm,
A soft glow shimmers like a secret.
The abyss, vast and seemingly endless,
Hums with a quiet inner light.

Dark walls pulse with hidden warmth,
Each crevice cradling a luminous spark.
The void is not merely darkness,
But a canvas for fragile hope.

Peering into the radiant abyss,
One sees scattered fragments of truth.
They flicker like distant fireflies,
Illuminating corners of despair.

A delicate beam of light emerges,
Challenging the notion of absolute darkness.
In its soft glow, despair dissolves
Into whispers of possibility and renewal.

The chasm breathes a surreal magic,
Where every shadow holds a hidden gleam.
It teaches that even in emptiness,
A spark of life quietly persists.

The abyss becomes a mirror of the soul,
Reflecting both sorrow and untold wonder.
Its radiant fragments invite the seeker
To find beauty within the void.

Every flicker of light inspires courage,
A call to embrace the unexpected.
Hope resides in the heart of darkness,
Nurtured by the glow of resilience.

Here, in this mysterious depth,
The balance of night and light is revealed.
The radiant abyss whispers its secret:
Even in darkness, life sings softly.

"अब इस गहरी खाई में,
हर अंधकार के कोने में एक नया प्रकाश छिपा है,
जहाँ वीरता की कहानी धीरे-धीरे उभरती है,
और हर झिलमिलाहट में आशा की किरण चमकती है।
यहाँ, सूनी दीवारें भी अपनी पुरानी यादों से गूंजती हैं,
प्रकृति के हर स्पंदन में जीवन का संदेश मिलता है,
हर बूंद में पुनरुत्थान का वादा छिपा है,
और इस शांत परछाई में आत्मा की गहराई
और नवजीवन का आह्वान सुनाई देता है।"

36. The Shattered Halo

Once, in a realm of light,
A perfect halo crowned a divine soul,
A symbol of unblemished grace
And innocence, shining bright.
But fate, in its course, shattered
That flawless ring—
Its gleaming circle broken
Into fragments on cold, hard ground.
Each shard lay silent,
A relic of lost perfection and purity,
A testament to a fall from grace
And the burden of broken dreams.

The fragments glimmered faintly
Under a somber sky,
Whispering memories
Of an innocence long forgotten.
Every sliver held echoes
Of laughter and tears,
A record of youthful hope
Marred by time's cruel hand.
They became silent reminders
Of lessons learned
Through the harsh light of lived heartache.

A solitary wanderer,
Burdened by scars,
Discovered the shattered relic,
Drawn by a magnetic pull
To fragments of a lost celestial crown.
They knelt among the remnants,
Eyes wide with sorrow and wonder,
Feeling each piece mirror
Their fractured past.
In that quiet moment,
The wanderer saw
Not merely broken beauty,
But a call to mend
The fragments of their soul.

Gently, they gathered each fragment
With tender care,
Polishing the pieces
With the healing touch
Of a wounded heart.
As the shards came together,
Transformation stirred within—
What was once despair
Evolved into a mosaic of redemption.
In that act of repair,
A newfound strength emerged,

A realization that beauty
Rises from the ruins of brokenness.

With each restored piece,
The halo began to shine anew,
Reborn with scars of wisdom.
The renewed halo radiated
A deep, resilient light,
Illuminating paths ahead
With hope forged in adversity.
Its glow spoke of resilience
And the promise of renewal,
A beacon urging lost souls
To mend and soar again.

Now, the restored halo whispers
Of mended fractures and hidden grace.
Its light carries echoes
Of what was broken and rebuilt.
The wanderer finds solace
In this sacred emblem of transformation,
Where every scar is a stroke
Of resilience painted in radiant hues.
The halo stands not as a reminder
Of past failures,
But as a luminous guide
Towards endless redemption.

In the stillness after chaos,
Each fragment sings of rebirth—
A soft chorus of hope
Echoing through the void.
The broken pieces, now aligned,
Reveal a secret strength
That outshines the darkness
Of former despair.

Beneath the starlit vault,
The halo becomes a mirror
Of every brave heart
That dared to rebuild itself.
In its fractured light,
We find reflections
Of courage, grace,
And relentless will—
An eternal promise
Of transformation.

The shattered halo now pulses
With a quiet, cosmic rhythm,
As if each restored shard
Beats in sync with the universe.
It speaks of wounds that heal
And scars that glitter like jewels,

Reminding us that every end
Ushers in a radiant new beginning.

"अब इस टूटे-फूटे नूर में छुपा है एक नया संदेश,
हर टुकड़ा कहता है जीवन की नई कहानी,
जहाँ दर्द के साथ मिलती है समझ की रोशनी,
और हर निशाँ बन जाती है आशा की किरण।
यह क्षण पुनर्जागरण का मधुर गीत गाता है,
हर टूटन में उमंग की नई लहर जगाता है,
और हर आहट में गूँजता है अनंत सौंदर्य।
हर अंश में बसती है हमारी आत्मा की गहराई,
जो हर मोड़ पर हमें मजबूत बनाती है,
और हर क्षण में उजाले की एक नई दस्तक देती है।"

37. The Veins of the Earth

Deep beneath rugged peaks, the Earth pulses,
Its ancient heartbeat resonating in hidden depths.
Veins of molten hope run like rivers,
Carving through stone and soil with fervour,
A slow, relentless surge of life and sorrow,
Whispering secrets of time's eternal passage.

In the labyrinth of rock and root,
Crimson currents flow with quiet intensity,
Each vein a thread of vibrant energy,
Mingling molten desire with buried grief.
They trace the scars of a long-forgotten past
And illuminate the mysteries of nature's soul.

We stand as echoes of this primordial rhythm,
Our emotions intertwined with Earth's deep pulse.
Like fragile hearts pulsing with ancient streams,
We feel the warmth of hope and the chill of loss,
Bound by nature's enduring, steady cadence,
A reminder that our pain and passion are one.

The Earth's veins speak of resilience and renewal,
Carrying the memory of life through the ages.
They bear unspoken dreams and silent tears,

Each glowing thread a symbol of enduring strength,
Revealing the delicate dance of light and shadow,
Where sorrow gives way to a promise of rebirth.

Amid these currents, a transformative force unfolds—
Nature's embrace mends what time has weathered.
In the quiet between each pulsing vein,
A luminous energy stirs,
Filling the void with the promise of new beginnings
And igniting our inner spark with fierce, raw beauty.

In the quiet solitude of nature's core,
Every tremor in the ground mirrors our inner stirrings.
We sense deep connection between our souls and land,
Each heartbeat a reflection of Earth's timeless rhythm.
A symphony composed in the language of stone and fire,
Binding human emotion to the pulse of existence.

Time flows like a river through these living veins,
Transforming pain into lessons of gentle endurance.
The Earth, in its majestic silence, reveals our truth:
That beauty often emerges from hidden, tender wounds,
Where ancient energy meets fleeting grace,
We find solace in nature's relentless, renewing embrace.

In this vast, living tapestry, nature sings its story;
Every rock and root holds echoes of our own hearts.

The Earth's pulse becomes our pulse—a pure connection,
An invitation to heal, to grow, and to understand,
That our emotions, like its molten veins, endure,
Carving paths of hope through the landscape of time.

"अब इस धरती की गहराई में,
हर नस में छिपा है अनंत जीवन का राज़,
जहाँ दर्द और खुशी का संगम मिलता है,
और हर स्पंदन गाथा सुनाता है पुनरुत्थान की।
इस मिट्टी की खुशबू में बसी है सच्ची उम्मीद,
हर बूंद में छुपा है नया उजाला,
और हर पल में खिलता है अटूट प्रकाश,
हर क्षण हमें सिखाता है जीने की नई राह,
जीवन के इस सुर में गूंजती है अनंत दास्ताँ,
और हर सांस में बसती है हमारी आत्मा की पराकाष्ठा।"

38. The Shrouded Horizon

The horizon lies shrouded in a veil of mist,
A distant border of soft light and deep shadow,
Its blurred edges whisper secrets of possibility,
Hinting at worlds beyond our immediate grasp,
A promise of beginnings veiled in uncertainty.

A solitary traveller stands at the edge,
Heart heavy with questions and quiet hope,
Gazing into the mysterious distance with longing,
Unsure of what awaits in the unknown lands,
Yet drawn forward by the lure of unseen paths.

Footsteps echo on a winding, shadowed trail,
The air is rich with the scent of rain and earth,
Each step carries both trepidation and gentle thrill,
As the traveller ventures into twilight's soft embrace,
Meditating on the balance of risk and reward.

In the soft glow of dawn, the mist begins to part,
Revealing hints of colour and a promise of new light,
The once-hidden horizon slowly unveils its secret,
Each ray sings a quiet ode to transformation,
Whispering that renewal dwells in mystery.

The traveller feels a stirring deep within the soul,
A quiet certainty amidst the shifting veils,
Embracing the unknown and stepping into change,
For every ending births a fresh, vibrant start,
Their journey a testament to hope's enduring power.

The shrouded horizon becomes a mirror of life,
Reflecting both uncertainty and the promise of dawn,
In its mystic depths, dreams and fears intertwine,
Guiding the traveller toward a destiny uncharted,
A story of potential and profound transformation.

"अब इस धुंधली सीमांत रेखा में,
जहाँ हर सुबह का वादा अनजानी उम्मीदों में डूबा है,
हर एक कदम पर खुलते हैं अनदेखे रास्ते,
जो दिल की गहराइयों से निकलते हैं।
हर मोड़ पर बुनती है ज़िंदगी नई दास्ताँ,
जहाँ अनिश्चितता में भी चमकती है उम्मीद की लौ,
हर सांस में बसता है खुद की खोज का असर,
और हर पल में मिलती है आत्मा की अनमोल पहचान।"

39. The Silent Chorus

In the vast amphitheatre, stone walls murmur secrets,
Their cold surfaces whisper lost laughter and despair.
Silence holds echoes of voices long stilled.
Shadows dance softly as the past awakens in harmony.
The empty stage sings a hymn of vivid memories,
Beneath the fading light, history breathes anew.

A chorus of silent voices rises from the cold stone,
Each note is a fragile thread woven with shared pain.
Unspoken sorrow and hidden joy merge in the quiet.
Their harmony binds lonely hearts with subtle strength.
The echo of memory becomes a timeless refrain,
In every reverberation, the soul finds solace.

Some echoes are gentle, like soft murmurs on a breeze,
Others resound deeply, reverberating in ancient arches.
Together they form a tapestry of forgotten dreams.
Every sound bears the weight of unvoiced experience.
The silent symphony unites all who listen with empathy,
Their resonant whispers mend the fractures of solitude.

In this hallowed silence, past and present converge,
The amphitheater transforms into an archive of longing.
Unspoken memories bloom like delicate flowers at dusk.

Each murmur reminds us of shared loss and quiet hope.
Loneliness fades into a soulful celebration of life,
While time pauses here, cradling each recollection.

The chorus rises and falls like the ocean's timeless tide,
Each surge reflects the myriad emotions of hearts.
The unity of these voices kindles a quiet resolve.
Their resonance inspires us to honour every story.
In every silent note, strength to persevere is found,
As the melody swells, it renews the spirit of the crowd.

Every whisper and soft murmur testifies to resilience,
The echo of voices transcends the bounds of solitude.
They invite us to listen deeply to tales etched in stone.
This collective song nurtures hope and understanding.
It guides us toward compassion and renewed inner light,
Within its cadence, we discover the power to heal.

"अब इस वीरान रंगमंच पर, हर पत्थर अपनी कहानी बयान करता है,
जहाँ हर धुन में दर्द और खुशी का अनोखा संगम समाया है।
हर खामोशी में एक मधुर अनकही बात झलकती है,
जो दिलों को बाँधती है हमारी साझा यादों की लय से।
हर स्वर में गूँजती है अनंत प्रेम की गाथा,
जैसे हर बूंद में छुपा हो जीवन का सच्चा सार।
इस अदृश्य धारा में, हम अपने भीतर के उजाले पाते हैं,
और हर पल में गहराई से उभरता है अनंत आत्म-साक्षात्कार।"

40. The Whispering Fog

In a forgotten valley, soft fog veils the land.
Grey mists drift gently over ancient, silent stones.
Each wisp murmurs secrets of days past.
Hidden truths float like whispers on the breeze.
The valley guards mysteries beneath a quiet shroud.

Fog weaves through gnarled trees and crumbling walls.
Cold mist softens echoes of faded, distant pain.
Every tendril carries memories of forgotten lore.
Whispers of old dreams stir beneath the haze.
Time pauses in the tender embrace of fog.

Deep within the mist, shadow and light entwine.
The valley emerges as secrets slowly take shape.
Mystery and clarity dance with each soft step.
Faint glimmers reveal fragments of hidden truth.
Each breath holds promise amid shifting fog.

As the fog lifts, the valley turns to gentle gold.
Soft light reveals contours of a long-lost dream.
Ancient ruins glisten under a tender, glowing sky.
Renewed life awakens from the mist's retreat.
The quiet scene sings a hymn of renewal.

The fog recedes, unveiling streams of clear water.
Nature awakens from a long, hidden sleep.
Misty breath nurtures tender blooms in silence.
Every new ray unveils a new secret wonder.
Hope rises like dawn after deep darkness.

In the cleared air, echoes of old dreams stir.
Every sound becomes a call for new growth.
The valley sings a soft, vibrant hymn.
Truth and beauty blend in calm unity.
A promise of clarity shines amid the peace.

"अब इस घाटी में उजाले की नई उमंग जगती है,
हर धुँध के पीछे पुरानी कहानियाँ गूंजती हैं,
हर बूंद में छुपी है गहरी यादों की परत,
हर किरण में मिलता है नयी आशा का संदेश,
हर लहर में बसी है आत्मा की अनकही सच्चाई,
ये सन्नाटा खोलता है मन के अनदेखे राज़,
और दिल में जगमगाता है नवजीवन का प्रतिज्ञान।"

41. The Flickering Ember

In the cold darkness of a desolate night,
A solitary ember flickers with quiet defiance.
Its soft glow defies the bitter chill,
A tiny flame that whispers of unyielding hope,
Lighting the void with a spark of persistent courage.

A lone traveller wanders through the gloom,
Eyes drawn to that gentle, unwavering light.
The ember shimmers like a beacon of fragile strength,
Its steady pulse a reminder that hope endures,
Even when the world is cloaked in endless night.

This small flame, though modest in size,
Holds within it the promise of renewal and life.
Each flicker tells a tale of battles fought in silence,
A testament to resilience amid overwhelming odds,
A defiant whisper that light persists through despair.

The ember's glow casts dancing shadows on stone.
It transforms darkness into a canvas of light.
Its gentle radiance softens solitude's cold edges.
It invites the traveller to pause and reflect.
And to embrace the enduring power of quiet strength.

In solitary light, the traveller finds solace,
A silent assurance that even small hope inspires,
The ember becomes a mirror for their quiet resolve,
A symbol that from deepest night, light always emerges,
And every heart holds the power to overcome.

Emboldened by the flame, the traveller steps on,
Carrying the ember's resolve as a sacred talisman,
Each step is fuelled by persistent hope,
A promise to nurture light within their soul,
And to let that glow guide them through life's trials.

As the night slowly yields to the first hints of dawn,
The ember's glow remains a steadfast, gentle reminder—
That in every moment of despair, hope quietly burns on,
Igniting the spirit to rise, to dream, to endure,
And lighting the path toward a future reborn.

"अब इस अंधेरी रात में भी जलता है एक छोटा चिराग,
जिसकी मधुर लौ में बसती है अनंत उम्मीद की कहानी।
हर पल ये दिखाता है कि निराशा में भी होता है उजाला,
और हर दिल में छुपी होती है, अटल साहस की शान।
ये चिराग हमें याद दिलाता है, कि रोशनी हमेशा जीतती है।"

42. The Mariner's Compass

Night drapes the ship like a whispered secret,
And on its creaking deck, a mariner stands,
Caught between fading memories and distant horizons.
Starlight glitters on the waves, offering faint comfort,
Yet his eyes return to a peculiar compass in hand,
Defying north to follow the hidden pull of his heart.

In the quiet between stars and waves,
A secret pulse of time softly whispers,
Dreams of lost voyages stir beneath the deep,
Hope and despair mingle in the salt-laced air,
Each ripple carries the silent weight of forgotten tales,
The sea cradles echoes of ancient promises,
And night's hush sings a hymn of destiny.

Every tilt of the needle echoes unspoken longing.
The observer, from a discreet distance, almost feels
A current of unseen energy drawing him forward.
While most seek magnetic bearings,
He chases the intangible,
As if pursuing a shore no map has ever charted.

Now and then, the mariner gazes over the railing,
Lost in the hush of rolling tides.

One can sense memories stirring in the lines on his face,
Fragments of distant harbours, letters never sent,
And a deep-rooted ache for a place he cannot name.
The compass trembles in his grip,
Urging him to trust mystery.

A restless wind gathers, and the sails groan in protest.
Clouds blot out the moon, casting the deck in shadow.
Thunder rumbles, a low warning from the horizon,
Yet the mariner stands resolute—
A quiet defiance that the observer can't help but admire,
For it takes courage to follow a call no one else can hear.

Lightning cleaves the sky in a sudden blaze,
Revealing in the mariner's eyes fear and determination.
He holds the compass, its glow steadfast against storm,
And in that brief flash, it's as though the entire sea
Is conspiring to test his resolve,
Demanding he prove his faith in an unseen destination.

Eventually, the tempest relents,
Leaving the air thick with the memory of thunder.
Seawater drips from sails and from the mariner's brow,
But the compass needle remains unwavering—
Pointing somewhere beyond the known,
Toward a promise only he perceives.

At dawn, the sky unfurls in rose and gold,
Exposing a calm that feels almost otherworldly.
He stands near the prow, exhaustion lining his features,
Yet there is a new softness in his gaze—
A sense that "home" might be less a faraway port
And more a quiet acceptance that he carries within.

"उसकी मंज़िल नक़्शों पर दर्ज नहीं, फिर भी दिल में जगती है,
सागर के हर थपेड़े में उसके हौसले की कहानी लिखी जाती है।
ये कंपास, जो धड़कनों की दिशा दिखाता है,
उसे सिखा रहा है कि घर कोई ठिकाना नहीं—
बल्कि एक एहसास है, जो मंज़िल से पहले ही मिल जाता है।"

43. The Solitary Beacon

On a rugged cliff by the stormy sea,
A lone lighthouse stands steadfast and proud.
Its weathered walls and flickering light
Speak of resilience in the face of isolation.

Amid the howling winds and crashing waves,
Its unwavering beam cuts through the dark,
A piercing glow of hope and guidance
That defies the loneliness of its perch.

The beacon shines as a steadfast signal,
Drawing lost souls back from the tumult,
Offering direction in a world adrift,
Where isolation often clouds the heart.

Though the lighthouse stands solitary,
Its light reaches far beyond its walls,
Touching distant shores and weary travellers,
Reminding them that guidance is always near.

Every flash of its radiant beam
Is a silent promise of renewal and strength,
An inner light that burns even in solitude,
Beckoning those adrift to find their way.

In the vast expanse of the restless sea,
The beacon bridges despair and hope,
A symbol that even in isolation,
Our inner light can guide us home.

Its glow is a quiet call to the wandering,
A reminder that no soul is truly alone,
For every heart holds a spark of brilliance,
Waiting to shine through the darkest night.

Standing as a guardian against the storm,
The solitary beacon nurtures lost dreams,
Offering a steady hand in turbulent times,
A radiant promise that direction endures.

"इस सुनसान तट पर, एक दीपस्तंभ खड़ा है,
जिसकी रौशनी अंधेरों को चीरती है।
हर चमक में छुपा है आशा का संदेश,
जो खोए दिलों को नई राह दिखाता है।
अकेलेपन में भी, वह उजाला बरसाता है,
और बयान करता है कि सच्चा विश्राम
हमारे भीतर ही छिपा होता है।"

44. The Electric Echo

Under the electric glow of a restless city,
I wandered into an abandoned data centre,
Where screens flickered with ghostly remnants,
And a lone beep echoed like a heartbeat
From a time when machines sang with life.

I followed the sound through corridors lined with tech,
Dusty servers and gadgets whispered memories,
Fragments of laughter, conversations coded in silence,
As if the building remembered passion and connection.
Now reduced to echoes in the modern dark.

In a forgotten room, images danced on cracked walls,
Flickering data merged into scenes of joy and tears.
Old code pulsed with the warmth of human touch,
Illuminating moments when technology united hearts,
A soft glow born from the energy of past dreams.

The echo swelled into a chorus of lost voices,
Not of sorrow, but of hope and resilient light,
The silent archive of circuitry and memory spoke,
Revealing that even in decay, connection endures,
Transforming emptiness into a sanctuary of renewal.

I sat before a terminal, its screen a mosaic of data,
Every pixel shimmered with promise of beginnings,
The echo invited me to listen to its coded lullaby,
To piece together stories of lives intertwined with tech,
And find that every byte carried a spark of eternal hope.

Leaving the data center, the hum lingered in my mind,
A constant reminder that even in urban desolation,
The spirit of connection pulses beneath the surface,
In this world of silent networks and hidden code,
Hope waits, ever ready to be rediscovered.

"अब इस सुनसान तकनीकी अड्डे में,
जहाँ हर स्क्रीन पर छुपी है यादों की झलक,
हर धुन में गूँजता है प्रेम का संदेश,
और हर पल में खिलती है नई आशा की सरगम।
यह विद्युत गूँज बताती है कि जुड़ाव की रोशनी
ना कभी मुरझाती है, ना धुंधली पड़ती है;
ये फिर से जगमगा उठती है,
जैसे अंधेरे में भी उजाले का एक नया सवेरा उभरता है।"

45. The Veil of Solace

In the heart of a forgotten urban garden,
A thin veil of mist drapes softly over cracked concrete,
Blurring harsh lines between rust and reclaimed nature,
It whispers of hidden oases amid the city's clamour,
A silent promise of comfort waiting to be discovered,
It invites the seeker into a quiet retreat.

Woven from the breath of early dawn and dreams,
The veil shimmers with traces of memories and hope,
It drapes over neglected parks and abandoned murals,
Softening the rigid edges of a bustling, indifferent world,
Inviting weary souls to pause and rediscover their light,
A gentle veil that transforms chaos to calm.

A solitary wanderer, burdened by daily struggles,
Steps into this sanctuary with cautious wonder,
Each footfall is a prayer, a moment of introspection,
As the veil wraps around him like a gentle embrace,
Dimming the noise of the city to a murmur of peace,
In its silence, the heart finds respite.

Beneath the mist, his thoughts drift like leaves,
Merging with the soft hum of wind and urban echoes,
Every step becomes a meditation—a chance to heal,

As the veil transforms chaos into a canvas of renewal,
Where every shadow reveals a spark of strength,
Nature's breath restores the weary spirit.

Deeper in the mist, wonders begin to emerge:
A hidden garden bursting with resilient wildflowers,
Graffiti that tells stories of defiant hope and rebirth,
Silent corners that echo with the laughter of dreams,
Each sight a reminder that beauty thrives in resilience,
Every vision blooms with quiet promise.

By the time the veil lifts, a gentle glow fills the space,
Illuminating a path where pain has softened into grace,
The wanderer, now filled with a sense of purpose,
Realizes that solace is found in embracing vulnerability—
A delicate balance of letting go and rising anew,
A new chapter awakens with each step.

"अब इस बिखरी हुई दुनिया में,
जहाँ हर कोने में छुपा है दर्द का अँधेरा,
एक नरम परदा बिछा देता है नई राह,
जहाँ हर कदम में झलकती है पुनर्जागरण की रौशनी,
और आत्मा में बसता है गहरी शांति का संदेश,
जहाँ खोई हुई उम्मीदों की फिर से छाप उभरती है,
हर सांस में जगमगाती है अनंत संभावनाओं की झलक,
और दिल में भर देती है जीने की नयी उमंग।"

46. The Twilight Oracle

At the junction of day and night,
A soft glow lingers on the horizon,
Fading daylight meets emerging starlight,
And the sky hums a quiet, transitional hymn,
Marking the delicate pause between two worlds.

From this sacred twilight, a mystical figure appears,
A silent oracle clothed in dusk and dawn,
Its presence is ethereal, barely touching the air,
An enigmatic guide emerging from the in-between,
Whispering secrets of change to those who listen.

Its voice is a blend of fading warmth
And newborn brilliance,
A harmony of soft, golden rays
And the cool glimmer of stars,
Every word resonates with ancient wisdom
And fresh hope, echoing beauty and promise.

The oracle speaks in cryptic verses of time and fate,
Inviting seekers to embrace the art of transition,
It tells of journeys where every loss births new light,
And every ending is but a prelude to transformation,
A call to see change as a vital, renewing force.

In the quiet after its sacred words,
A profound calm settles over the twilight.
Each breath becomes a silent prayer
For paths yet undiscovered and dreams unspoken,
The fading light deepens, revealing hidden pathways,
Where uncertainty transforms into renewal.

As the oracle's murmurs fade into the vast expanse,
A cosmic echo stirs within the heart of the night.
A timeless rhythm awakens deep inside,
Resonating with the pulse of distant galaxies.
It invites each wanderer to delve beyond the seen,
To uncover the luminous truths hidden in silence.

Its advice is a mirror reflecting life’s impermanence,
Urging hearts to let go of the familiar
And step boldly into the unknown,
To trust that between what was and what will be
Lies an infinite reservoir of wisdom and renewal,
A quiet invitation to dance with change.

In this twilight, the oracle reveals truth is fluid,
That shadow of yesterday dissolves into light,
It reminds us wisdom is born in these spaces,
Where deepest fears and brightest hopes intertwine,
And every word sparks a new beginning within.

The dance of dusk and dawn becomes a lesson,
An reminder that nothing stays fixed in time,
Each moment is a doorway to self-discovery,
Where the old fades and the new emerges,
Carrying with it the promise of growth, rebirth.

"अब इस संध्या में छुपा है ज्ञान का अनमोल ख़ज़ाना
जहाँ हर धूप और छाँव मिलकर रचते हैं एक नई कहानी,
इस मधुर पल में झलकते हैं परिवर्तन के गूढ़ राज़
जो दिल को खोलकर देते हैं अटल उम्मीदों का संदेश
हर साँस में बसी है जीवन की नई रौशनी
और हर लम्हा गूंजता है अनंत परिवर्तन के संगीत से
जैसे समय स्वयं अपने आप में एक नए सवेरा का वादा करता हो।"

47. The Storm of Solitude

A violent storm roars overhead,
Winds whip and thunder shakes the sky,
Amid chaos, one solitary figure stands,
Defiant against nature's raging fury,
Eyes fixed on the tempest's heart,
Their stance, a quiet act of rebellion.

Rain pelts like a thousand tears,
Lightning splits the darkened heavens,
The storm mirrors inner chaos and doubt,
A wild, unbridled force of emotion,
Each gust echoing restless memories,
Every flash revealing raw vulnerability.

In isolation, the figure finds strange beauty,
The fury of the storm becomes a mirror,
Reflecting a soul battered yet unbroken,
Every drop of rain sings a note of survival,
Amid the tumult, hope flickers like embers,
A silent testament to resilience.

The swirling tempest is a metaphor
For inner turmoil and fierce self-doubt,
A clash of anger, fear, and longing,

Yet in the chaos, truth quietly emerges,
The storm challenges the spirit to evolve,
For in solitude, raw beauty is born.

Defiant and still, the figure endures,
Their heart beats in sync with the raging rain,
They learn to embrace the harsh winds,
Finding grace in wild disorder,
Each moment of isolation carves strength,
And every crashing wave molds self-acceptance.

As the storm rages on, transformation unfolds,
The relentless force devastates and refines,
In isolation, pain becomes a catalyst for change,
And turmoil gives way to inner clarity,
The tempest teaches that solitude is dual-natured,
Both tumultuous and remarkably transformative.

In the echo of crashing waves, a testimony emerges,
A story penned in tears and fervent dreams,
The ocean's roar speaks of a soul that loved fiercely,
Yet in its eternal cycle lies the promise of renewal,
A reminder that every tumultuous moment
Offers a chance to rise anew.

In quiet lull after the storm, reflections whisper softly,
The figure surveys the landscape reshaped by fury,

New paths of understanding etch themselves within,
Each mark a guide for future trials,
A gentle assurance that every storm imparts wisdom,
Carving out hope in the heart of chaos.

Within solitude, clarity blossoms like spring buds,
The aftermath of chaos nurtures a tender inner calm,
The soul learns to cherish the scars and the strength,
Embracing life fully, even amidst lingering tempests,
Where the darkest hours yield seeds of luminous hope,
And renewal emerges from the depths of despair.

"अब इस तूफ़ानी अकेलेपन में,
उभरता है जीवन का तेज़ उजाला,
जहाँ हर आंधी में छुपा है अनमोल संदेश,
स्वयं को जानने की राह, अद्भुत और पवित्र।
इस निरंतर गर्जना में, दर्द और साहस मिलते हैं,
हर बूँद में ढलती है नई उम्मीद की कहानी,
दिल खोलकर महसूस होती है हर लहर की गूंज,
और अंधेरों में भी खिल उठता है एक मधुर प्रकाश।"

48. The Spark of Reminiscence

Deep in a dark, ancient forest,
A solitary spark glows with quiet fire.
It smoulders softly amid shadowed trees,
A cherished memory that endures,
Refusing to fade into the night,
Its light a tender, constant reminder.
This glowing spark, small yet profound,
Carries the warmth of forgotten days,
A fragment of passion from times long past,
It burns with the hues of deep amber,
Illuminating a piece of the soul,
A fragment of hope that persists,
The spark casts a gentle, golden glow,
Painting the forest floor with soft light,
Each flicker unveils hidden corners of memory.

As if whispering secrets of bygone laughter,
A silent story of love and loss,
Etched in the delicate flames of remembrance,
Its radiant warmth invites quiet reflection,
Drawing wanderers to pause and listen,
In the flickering light, the past comes alive,
Every flicker kindles a yearning for renewal,

A moment to embrace both joy and sorrow,
Transforming solitude into a sacred space,
The spark's glow dances with the night,
Casting silhouettes of forgotten dreams,
It weaves a tapestry of soft nostalgia,
Blurring the line between memory and desire,
Each flicker celebrates a quiet triumph,
A luminous whisper of life's enduring beauty.

The spark bridges yesterday with today,
Linking tender memories with the present moment,
Its glow stirs the heart with gentle resolve,
Illuminating pathways once shrouded in darkness,
Each flicker a call to find inner strength,
A reminder that hope endures through time,
Amid the quiet of the forest, the spark burns,
A beacon of resilient beauty in the gloom,
It teaches that even the smallest light
Can cast away the deepest shadows,
And that every memory holds power to inspire,
Fuelling the soul with renewed possibility,
In this enchanted solitude, the past softly sings,
A delicate hymn of moments cherished and lost,
The spark's glow weaves a tapestry of dreams.

Where every flame is a promise of new beginnings,
A timeless dialogue between heart and nature,

Carrying the eternal spark of life's mystery,
Whispered winds carry tales of yore,
Where every shadow cradles a secret,
Moonlit leaves sing songs of solace,
And ancient boughs remember lost lullabies,
The quiet earth cradles dreams untold,
In the stillness, hearts find gentle reprieve,
Sparks of passion kindle the silent night,
Their glow echoes with the promise of dawn,
Each spark a verse in nature's endless song,
Mysteries unfold in the hush of twilight,
In the dance of light, hope and memory entwine,
Illuminating the path to tomorrow's grace.

"अब इस अंधेरे वन में,
एक अंगीठी सी याद जलती है,
जिसकी मधुर लौ में बीते कल की अनकही कहानी छुपी है,
हर झिलमिलाहट में खिलता है नई आशा का उजाला।
हर साये में छुपा होता है अमर प्रेम का पैगाम,
जो सूखे पत्तों में भी जीवन का संकेत छोड़ जाता है,
हर बूंद में संजोए हैं दिल के गहरे अरमान,
और हर पल में बसी है एक अनंत, प्रबल रोशनी। "

49. The Woven Fates

Within the silent cosmos, an immense loom glows
Beneath a blanket of starlight.
Ancient strands stretch into endless night,
Each filament holds a life—
A tale of joy, sorrow, and dreams,
Spun by fate's timeless hand.

Delicate threads glisten like soft murmurs
Of memories from ages past.
They weave a graceful ballet of destiny,
Carving paths of passion and surrender,
Bearing the weight of promises
Never spoken aloud.

Across the vast expanse, threads wander and converge,
Each intersection a silent tribute
To intertwined lives and shared fates.
The cosmic tapestry unfolds slowly,
Painting every life as a vital hue,
A mosaic where no soul stands alone.

Here, chance and purpose entwine in a dance,
Random encounters become eternal bonds.
A gentle murmur of fate binds hearts and dreams,

Reminding us that even the smallest life
A spark of connection lights the unseen,
Adds brilliance to the whole.

As shimmering strands twist and coil,
Destinies reveal themselves in every knot.
Each twist echoes tales of love and grief,
The fabric of existence pulses with hidden rhythm,
Where every subtle line sings
A part of an eternal song.

The universe's loom spins in constant motion,
Every glimmer on a thread recalls triumph and despair.
Amid chaos and order, the tapestry grows richer,
Threads of destiny interlace in silent wonder,
Embracing the unpredictable beauty
Of each unique human journey.

Individual paths merge into this grand design,
Each thread—delicate or bold—enriches the picture.
A map of interconnected souls unfolds,
A timeless reminder that our lives
In every strand, our stories intertwine,
Form part of an eternal cosmic saga.

Within the cosmic tapestry, whispers of unity arise,
As vibrant threads harmonize in a silent symphony.

Each individual note merges into a grand chorus,
A melody of shared destiny that resounds
Through the infinite void, gently echoing
That every life is a vital chord in the eternal song.

Bathed in the quiet glow of the starlit loom,
The tapestry unfurls slowly like a vivid chronicle.
Every heartbeat and silent tear
Each moment glimmers in the fabric of time,
Are captured in the interplay of chance and choice,
Affirming our collective, luminous essence.

"अब इस ब्रह्मांड की बुनाई में,
हर धागा एक नई दास्ताँ सुनाता है,
जहाँ प्रेम, दुःख और आशा का संगम मिलता है,
हर रेखा में जीवन की अनंत सच्चाई झलकती है,
और हर डोर पर छिपा है सपनों का अद्भुत संगम,
ये धागे हमारे अस्तित्व की गूढ़ कहानी बुनते हैं,
हर मोड़ पर मिलती है नई उम्मीद की चमक,
और हर चित्र में उजाला, जो हमें फिर से जोड़ता है।"

50. The Infinite Rebirth

Beneath a canvas of iridescent dawn,
Morning light spills like liquid jewels,
The world awakens in a riot of hue,
Crimson, gold, and turquoise merge,
A symphony of colour bursts forth,
Heralding the birth of a new day.

The air shimmers with untold promise,
Every breeze whispers uncharted potential,
Each heartbeat pulses with vibrant rhythm,
Drawing us closer to luminous dreams,
As if the world itself exhales hope,
And destiny glows in the early light.

Waves of radiant energy surge across horizons,
Carrying the delicate scent of wild blossoms,
Sun-kissed meadows sway in a gentle dance,
Nature composes an anthem of renewal,
Each petal and leaf sings its own refrain,
Painting the earth with life's fervent passion.

In the celebration of creation,
Mountains glisten with dewdrops like scattered gems,
Valleys bathe in the soft glow of reborn light,

Every step marks a bold brushstroke on fate's canvas,
The landscape transforms into a living masterpiece,
An eternal tribute to nature's resilient spirit.

Possibility unfurls in endless layers,
A tapestry woven from bold dreams and sparkling hope,
Even the faintest ray of sunlight ignites the soul,
Transforming the mundane into vibrant wonder,
Where each moment becomes a burst of creative life,
And every horizon whispers promises of tomorrow.

Amid this eternal cycle, life renews itself,
Old scars soften under the warmth of new beginnings,
The air vibrates with the pulse of transformation,
Resilience and renewal are etched in every stone,
A quiet fire kindles within our deepest being,
Illuminating the path to self-discovery.

The cosmos sings a hymn of endless change,
Celestial forces weave our shared destiny,
Every star reflects the echo of past triumphs,
Guiding our souls through the labyrinth of time,
In this boundless expanse, our hearts find their rhythm,
And the dance of life becomes our sacred truth.

With each dawn, the infinite rebirth unfolds,
Our spirit rises on wings of relentless hope,

The universe paints our dreams in hues of promise,
Every pulse of life is a celebration of renewal,
In the harmony of nature and time, we find our light,
And our journey continues—ever vibrant, ever new.

"अब इस अनंत पुनर्जागरण में,
हर सुबह एक नई रौशनी की बयार लाती है,
जहाँ हर पल में खिलता है अटल विश्वास,
हर धड़कन में बसी है उम्मीद की चमक,
हर कदम हमें ले जाता है उजाले की ओर,
यह पुनर्जागरण हमें सिखाता है,
कि हर नए सवेरे में छुपा है एक उत्सव,
और हर लम्हा है जीवन का अनंत संदेश।"

51. The Final Key

I began my journey on a winding path
Through the depths of my being.
Each step echoed silent lessons
From a storied past.
Old halos shattered; veiled truths guided me,
As whispers from a mirror urged me deeper within.

I wandered through forgotten corridors of time,
Where narrow alleys held keys
To triumphs and quiet resilience.
Every relic—be it brass, silver, or iron—
Spoke of battles fought
And moments of both piercing pain and profound grace.

In the ruins of memory, soft echoes rose,
Murmurs of the past interwoven with the present,
As long-lost dreams sang against cold walls.
They wove a tapestry of experience,
A blend of lessons transcending chaos,
Each thread a hymn of survival.

Beneath a vast, ever-changing sky,
A celestial veil of light and shadow unfurled,
Revealing fragments of forgotten ambition

Dancing upon rugged cliffs.
Each drop of hope cascaded like liquid dreams,
Illuminating a path where even darkness
Glitters with promise.

Within the storm of my inner world,
I discovered a truth both fierce and gentle:
The wildest storms nurture transformation.
Each struggle forged new strength in my heart,
Every pulse of raw emotion became
A stepping stone toward renewal,
Turning turmoil into a radiant beacon.

Then, amid the convergence of all these experiences,
A key emerged—luminous, ethereal, a light of insight.
Its gentle glow dissolved doubts
And rekindled forgotten dreams,
Opening not a door of stone but a gateway within,
Where self-realization intertwined with possibility.

In that transformative moment, I realized
The final key was never an object to be found,
But a spark that had always burned quietly inside me.
Every hardship, every joy,
Had shaped this inner luminescence—
Revealing that the answer to my quest
Was to embrace my true self.

Emboldened by this revelation, I stepped forward
With renewed purpose, guided by silent lessons
Etched in every scar and every memory.
Each challenge became a doorway;
Each scar, a symbol of rebirth,
As I navigated the intricate tapestry
Of my inner cosmos, where every experience
Merged into luminous truth.

The journey, once a solitary quest
Through dark, winding corridors,
Transformed into an odyssey of self-discovery and hope.
Every echo, every whisper of the past,
Became a vital piece of the mosaic that makes me whole.
A testament to inner strength and relentless growth.

"अब इस अंतिम चाबी में,
सभी अनुभवों का सार समाया है,
जहाँ हर दर्द ने रची है एक नई दास्ताँ,
और हर कदम ने उजाले की नई किरण जगाई है।
यह चाबी बताती है कि सच्ची रोशनी
हमारे भीतर ही निवास करती है,
और असली सफ़र वहीं से शुरू होता है—
जहाँ हर पल में मिलता है अनंत परिवर्तन का संदेश।"

9 789369 537693